LATERAL LEADERSHIP

Getting It Done
When You Are Not The Boss

Roger Fisher & Alan Sharp

With John Richardson,
Harvard Negotiation Project Editor

P
PROFILE BOOKS

1669644X

This second edition published in Great Britain in 2004 by
PROFILE BOOKS LTD
58A Hatton Garden
London EC1N 8LX
www.profilebooks.co.uk

First edition first published in Great Britain by HarperCollins, 1998

1 3 5 7 9 10 8 6 4 2

Printed and bound in Great Britain by
Bookmarque Ltd, Croydon, Surrey

A CIP catalogue record for this book is available from the British Library.

ISBN 1 86197 723 9

Contents

Preface to New Edition

The first UK edition of *Lateral Leadership* was substantially the same as that published by HarperBusiness under the title *Getting It DONE* in the USA.

In publishing a new UK edition, Profile Books have given us the opportunity to make some revisions and modifications. It would be odd if we believed the contents were incapable of improvement or clarification. We certainly do not. Nevertheless, the comments of readers encourage us to think that the ideas still stand up well. Therefore, we think it is too early for any substantial revision. We have made no changes in the body of the text, but attempt to respond in this edition to two important questions readers have raised. One concerns how the approach set out in this book relates to that set out in Roger's earlier co-authored book on negotiation. We deal with that in this new preface. The second question is how to start to apply the ideas in this book without taking too much risk. One way of limiting the risk perceived in any situation is to feel well prepared. In a new Appendix, we suggest how a reader might usefully prepare herself or himself to use the ideas in this book in their day-to-day working.

Lateral Leadership and Getting to YES

Readers have said it would be helpful to clarify the relationship between *Lateral Leadership* and Roger's earlier co-authored book *Getting to YES*. In the acknowledgments we refer to the differences of focus between Roger's and Alan's earlier work and the question they addressed in their work together. However, some further clarification is required.

Getting to YES points out that people negotiate something every day. They negotiate even when they don't think of themselves as doing so. Negotiation is a basic means of getting what you want. It is back-and-forth communication designed to reach an agreement when you and the other side have some interests that are shared and others that are opposed. Where there are disputes to be settled, differences to be resolved, the need to agree on terms for the exchange of goods or services, as in fixing the price of a product or conditions of employment, negotiation is a way of reaching an agreed outcome. In all such situations, you are likely to see yourself not as part of a group or team with the other parties with whom you are dealing but as on "the other side," part of a different group, or team. Therefore *Getting to YES* set out to answer the question: "What is the best way for people to deal with their differences; in particular what advice might we give one party that would help resolve the dispute more effectively for both?"

Yet, despite the broad definition of negotiation given above, you would not see every dealing that you have with others as a negotiation in the usual sense of that word. Nor, indeed, would it be helpful to do so. *Lateral Leadership* starts from the premise you have to work together with others to get things done every day. In some instances, you may see it as necessary to negotiate with another party to secure their agreement on the terms on which they will take part in the work. However, in most cases, as with colleagues working in the same organization, you would not see this as a prerequisite to starting to work together. People will have agreed to the terms on which they will do their job when they joined the organization. And a key part of their job *is* to collaborate with colleagues, bosses, and subordinates in getting things done to achieve the aims of the organization. They are starting from the point where they see themselves as part of the same group or team or organization with regard to what needs doing. To treat such dealings as a negotiation would be both frustrating and inefficient. For people who see themselves in such situations, *Lateral Leadership* set out to answer a different question: "What advice could we give one person — whatever his position — who wanted to make a group work more effectively?" By "group" we mean as few as two people who need to work together.

You have a dispute or difference which needs to be resolved. You need to agree on the terms for some exchange of goods or services, as in buying a house, or settling the salary and conditions of employment. You will want "to reach agreement without giving in," to avoid being "beaten" in some way by the other party. This leads often to an approach labeled "positional bargaining," which is adversarial in nature. The shortcomings of such an approach are described in *Getting to YES*, where the method of "principled negotiation" was put forward as a way of reaching agreement without giving in or being "beaten."

Where there are no terms to be agreed or disputes to be resolved, and the need is for collaboration to get things done, people are nevertheless often less than wholehearted or efficient in their efforts to work together. This is especially so until they get to know each other well. While the approach to each other is not usually adversarial, commonly a caution or wariness gets in the way of effective collaboration. Some individuals may be reluctant to contribute as much as they could in terms of ideas or effort, perhaps from fear that their ideas will be rejected or because "it's not my job." Conversely, others may be slow to encourage or invite contributions because they fear it may somehow weaken their own authority or status, "it's *my* job, not anyone else's, to provide the answers."

There are similarities in the two types of situation. Some people have compared a number of people trying to work together with a multiparty negotiation. In both you are concerned to move efficiently towards a satisfactory outcome. Nevertheless, there are important differences. In one you start on a different side; in the other you start as part of the same group. In one the outcome is an agreement; in the other the outcome is something gets done. A reader will have many examples of the two different sorts of dealings with the same people. For instance, you attend an interview for a job and need to negotiate the terms of employment with a prospective employer. Your main concern is how to arrive at an agreement that is in the interests of both parties and that you consider fair. Having done so, you take up the agreed post. Your concern now changes to how to collaborate effectively with your bosses, colleagues, and subordinates to achieve the aims of the organization you have joined. At some time in the future an issue or issues may arise where you feel you are not being treated fairly; for example, your responsibilities may increase to a point where you consider an increase in salary or wages would be justified. On this particular issue, you will be concerned, once again, to secure a mutually acceptable agreement, and the approach of "principled negotiation" is appropriate for this purpose. Nevertheless, in the many dealings you are still having with others in the course of your daily work, your concern remains one of how to collaborate effectively with others and how to promote collaboration among others. Here "lateral leadership" is appropriate.

There are many other situations where the parties may first need to agree on the terms on which things will be done, but subsequently the priority becomes one of collaborating effectively to get them done. A consultant negotiates the terms of an agreement with a client; he or she then needs to collaborate effectively with that client and to get that client to collaborate effectively with him or her to achieve the agreed objectives. The boards of directors of two companies negotiate the terms of a merger; they then have to work together and get their staffs to work together to achieve the objectives of the newly merged company. The parties in South Africa or Northern Ireland or Iraq negotiate the principles of a new constitution; they and their constituents need subsequently to collaborate effectively to make those principles work.

In the first phase in each of these examples it would not be helpful to apply the approach and methods described in this book. They are situations for which the method of "principled negotiation" described in *Getting to YES* was intended. Yet in all of these examples, once agreement has been reached that method is no longer as appropriate. Before agreement, it would be unwise for either party to assume that they were on the same side and had made the choice to help each other. Nor could you reasonably assume that the other party had revealed all the information they had that was relevant to working out an outcome. After agreement, it would be very inefficient if every attempt at collaborating to get things done were delayed by some negotiation over whether the parties would do so or not. It would also be incredibly frustrating if people always wanted to negotiate over whether they would contribute their thinking, ideas, and effort, or whether these would be accepted. And certainly it is not unreasonable to think that they should "choose to help." Yet there is often a need to overcome an apparent reluctance to contribute without persuasion and a reluctance to invite contribution for fear of losing control. In such situations, where the aim is effective collaboration to get things done, the method of "lateral leadership" described in this book is appropriate.

Key Questions

A question put frequently by anyone needing to negotiate is: "What if I have less power than the other party?" As those who have read it will know, *Getting to YES* provided an answer. A question posed even more frequently by anyone needing to work with others to get things done is: "What if I don't have the authority?" This book attempts to answer that question.

Alan Sharp
Roger Fisher
March 2004

Acknowledgments

This book took shape over some seven years. We have been using the ideas in it for decades. Over that time, many people have contributed to our thinking. We have refrained from extensive footnotes not to claim these ideas as original, but rather because we have adopted and used so much from so many that it is now impossible to sort out where everything came from. This note is to thank them all. Some require special mention.

We first met around the time that *Getting to YES* was published. We were introduced by Herb Behrstock of the United Nations Development Program, who had some experience with each of our work and felt that we might make a fruitful combination. Our first acknowledgment must be to Herb. Without him we would never have met, and this book would never have been written.

The focus of Roger's work had been the question, "What is the best way for people to deal with their differences?" In particular, "What advice might we give to one party that would help him resolve the dispute more effectively for both?" The answer was "Principled Negotiation," a practical method for negotiating agreement without giving in. The focus of Alan's work was the question, "What is the best advice we could give a number of people who are already on the same side who want to improve the way they work together so that they get high-quality results and feel that they have made the best use of their abilities?"

Together we considered a related question: "What advice could we give to one person — whatever his position — who wanted to make a group work more effectively?" Every day employees, bosses, colleagues, families, businesses, and nations face this same dilemma. To answer that question we put our respective experiences together to develop "Lateral Leadership," a method of leading "from the side" that can be used by anyone to nudge a group toward better performance. Both before and after we started to write the book we tried out the ideas on a wide range of people. We acknowledge with gratitude their comments and suggestions.

Alan wishes to record his great personal debt to the late Ralph Coverdale, who first gave him the opportunity to work in this field. The late Bernard Babington Smith was Alan's mentor for many years. Together these two men were the originators of Coverdale Training, and the original developers of many of the more important ideas contained in this book. Thanks are also due to Alan's Danish colleague Flemming Madsen, who worked for years with Alan on some of these ideas.

Chris Thorne spent more than a summer making sense out of our initial ideas and writing the first draft of a book, that after years of metamorphosis, became this book. While most of the words of that draft are gone, the effect of Chris's contribution is still found throughout.

Our sons, Kevin and Neil Sharp and Peter and Elliot Fisher, worked over and helped us with many of these ideas. We are grateful to them for continuing an interchange from which we continue to learn.

We would like to acknowledge the work of Ronald Heifetz,

director of the Leadership Education Project at the John F. Kennedy School of Government at Harvard University, who as a psychiatrist and a teacher of leadership has broken much of the ground on which we are working. We are grateful for his 1994 book, *Leadership Without Easy Answers,* which so nicely sharpens the distinction between authority and leadership.

Doug Stone has worked with both of us for years. At the beginning of this project, he spent long hours brainstorming ideas with us. At the end, he helped us by reading final drafts before the book went to the publisher. Throughout, he has been unfailingly encouraging.

Jeff Weiss of Conflict Management, Inc., read many drafts and gave us good advice. He taught a summer course at Harvard Law School based on the ideas in this book and helped us make them more accessible. It was always a pleasure to work with him.

Wayne Davis read several drafts and did a fine job of telling us what not to cut out. His enthusiasm and encouragement came at a time when we needed it. William Jackson, Roger's full-time assistant for several years before becoming a lawyer, contributed his energy, skills, and insights to this project while taking on many others as well.

Sheila Heen gave us ideas on making the text more readable and helped us to make the text sound less sexist. If there is anything left that sounds too old-fashioned, she probably tried to get us to change it.

The administrative assistant at the Negotiation Project, Lori Goldenthal, did countless hours of formatting and word processing. More important, she provided the best example of how someone without formal authority can give her bosses advice on how they ought to do things and have them be grateful. She has moved away from Cambridge, and we miss her.

Caroline Fisher was our hostess during long summers on Martha's Vineyard when much of the work was done. For years she and Marie Sharp put up with their husbands' desire to get these ideas down on paper. Their support was critical and is deeply appreciated.

Kirsten Sandberg, Dave Conti, and Janet Dery at Harper-Business all gave good advice on making the book more accessible. If these ideas get to more people as a result, we will have them to thank.

It is hard to find a word to describe the work John Richardson did on this book. That we wrote it "with" him may suggest that he is a ghostwriter who took our names and ideas and wrote the book himself. "Editor" suggests that he shaped and pared our writing but provided none of his own. John wrote first drafts of some chapters, rewrote drafts of ours, added stories and examples, and built on the framework of ideas. "Associate Author" may best describe his role. Thank you, John.

Roger
Alan
February 1998

Introduction: Why This Book?

This book is for you if you have ever found yourself frustrated trying in a disorganized way to get something done with others. You have probably experienced situations like the following:

JOE: I've been thinking about this job and I know exactly how to tackle it.

SALLY: Hang on. First I want to know why we are doing it.

JOE: That's obvious. The boss is dissatisfied with the present situation.

CHARLIE: Fair enough, but before we get started I want to get a timetable set up.

BILL: Okay. By when do we need to get the job done?

CHRISTINE: Before we sort that out, is anyone in charge of this job?

BILL: What you mean is that you think you should be in charge.

CHRISTINE: No, I don't. I'm just asking whether anyone is, and if not, whether someone should be.

JOE: I don't know about the rest of you, but I can't spend all day on this. I've got a lot of other things to do.

SALLY: I am still not sure what we are trying to do.

And so it goes until you make some sort of progress or run out of time. Most everybody departs complaining to themselves about how little has been achieved and what a waste of time it has been. You have probably been in a situation like this more times than you like to remember. That doesn't reflect badly on you. It is true for all of us.

Think about the preceding scene. What is it that this group needs? A common response is "leadership." "No wonder they can't get anything done. There is no one in charge." In our experience, leaders with authority can do many things, but producing better collaboration by fiat is not one of them.

This book is designed to help you get something done when you work with others. It is not about all the things that an authoritative leader can do, but what you can do. It is not about all possible goals, but about the goal of good collaboration — of getting results when you and others are working together. The skills of nudging your colleagues in the right direction are highly dependent on knowing a lot about the direction in which to nudge them.

There is an old railroad story of an expert being called in because a brand-new diesel locomotive would not start no matter what the engineer did. The expert arrived, studied the situation, and then gave the locomotive a light tap with a hammer. It started right up. When the railroad received the expert's bill for $1,000, they asked him to itemize it. The reply came:

- Hitting the locomotive with a hammer: $10
- Knowing where to hit it: $990

The task of stimulating good cooperation is similar. The precise step you take at the end is a minor part of the cure.

We suggest that whatever limits there may be on your official authority, you think of yourself as a potential leader. Time and again, you will find that you can change things for the better by using the skills of what we call "lateral leadership."

The goal of this book is to enable you to achieve high-quality collaboration with your colleagues — collaboration that produces high-quality results. You can do so, without authority over your coworkers, through lateral leadership. The method consists of three basic steps. The first step is to organize and sharpen your personal skills at getting things done by yourself. The second step is to understand clearly your strategic goal of an organized way of getting things done with others. The third step is learning some tactics of participatory leadership. You want to learn techniques by which you, as an equal member of a group, can ask, offer, and do things that stimulate others to become skillful at working together.

These three steps are like the steps taken by a jazz musician who wants to improve the way his combo sounds. First he needs to develop his skills at playing solo. Then he needs to understand the qualities of good jazz music played by a group — harmony, counterpoint, what sort of back-up playing makes the soloist sound better. Only then can he do things that lead his band mates to improve the way the group plays together.

We believe that you, or anyone else in a business, organization, committee, or other form of collaborative activity, can act in ways that will improve how you all work together to accomplish results.

PART A.
THE BIG PICTURE

1 GETTING IT DONE

Whoever you are, business executive, union member, staff support, consultant, or government official, you cannot accomplish all your goals by yourself. You need subordinates, coworkers, superiors, suppliers, or customers — people you depend on every day. Even a poet has to work with editors and publishers. Unless you are a hermit, there is no way you can get much done alone. So you work with others.

It turns out that collaboration is difficult. Robots on an assembly line are designed to work together with precision. People are not. Each of us has a mind of our own. And, unlike robots, each of us has feelings — of pleasure or anger, confidence or insecurity, friendship or jealousy. We also make judgments of what seems fair or unfair, right or wrong. As a result, when a number of us work together, it does not go easily.

TWO COMMON SYMPTOMS

Collaboration Is Poor

When working with others, most people get discouraged with how much effort is wasted. A level of cooperation is the product of a jumble of different approaches and ideas. Each one relies on experience, intuition, and habit. But all have different experiences, different intuitions, and different habits. The fact that individuals think differently can be a great resource. They can generate more ideas and approaches to choose from. Differences are also a burden. They make it hard for us to work together efficiently.

People waste time, misallocate their abilities, and come into conflict over and over again. Everyone has attended unproductive meetings that consume hours. We have found ourselves spending more time attempting to get organized than doing productive work. Trying to get things done with others can become so frustrating that most people have been tempted to undertake some burdensome task alone rather than put up with the hassle of organizing and implementing a joint effort.

And No One Is Making the Situation Better

When you stop to notice what you yourself are doing, it may not be encouraging. You discover that you, too, are not helping. Even when you want to help you rarely know how. If you say nothing, things don't improve. If you tell them to cooperate, things don't improve. If you point out how much time is being wasted, things don't improve. The more strongly you express your frustration, the more you become part of the problem.

You are smart enough to appreciate the time, effort, and emotion that are so often being squandered. The people you work with are, too. And if you are not making the collaboration more effective, neither are they. How come? This book explains why, and what you can do about it.

DIAGNOSIS: WE DON'T KNOW ENOUGH ABOUT GETTING THINGS DONE

There are at least three causes of a failure to improve collaboration — three problems that a person needs to solve before he or she has a chance to move a group toward better practices.

Personal Skills Are Limited

Even working alone, most of us are not experts on efficiency, and our coworkers know it. If we lack the skill of organizing the easiest case — working alone — how can we expect to be helpful in the more complex case of working with others?

We all know that there are times when we don't work very efficiently. Perhaps you are the sort of person who will drive around and around looking for an address rather than stop and ask directions. Perhaps you don't keep your checkbook balanced. You are probably not a model of perfect behavior at work, either. Do you find yourself jumping from one part of a task to another, picking something up, only to put it down and turn to something else?

And above all, people make similar mistakes again and again. An acquaintance of Alan's was in their local bar. In doing an impersonation of a famous pop star, he shot his arm into the air — and put it through the plaster of the low ceiling. A few days later he was in the same bar when a customer asked him how the damage had occurred. In explaining, he repeated his impersonation — and put his fist through the ceiling again! Like him, most of us could be better at learning from experience.

Too often our performance reflects a lack of good habits for getting things done. We do not have a simple system we can rely on to handle most of the situations we face. Neither do our colleagues. Since getting ourselves organized as individuals is more than most of us have succeeded in doing, it's no wonder that we haven't found better ways to get an office full of people working well together.

We Have No Clear Vision of What Good Collaboration Looks Like

Think for a moment. How would a group of us be behaving if we were cooperating effectively? What is that goal of good collaboration toward which you or somebody else should be trying to lead us?

This is a second explanation for a failure to improve the way that you and others get things done. You do not know what you want to bring about. Some people assume that cooperative behavior consists of being "nice" to one's fellow workers — being courteous, being friendly, and going along with their ideas. Being nice can help, but some of the "nicest" workers in the office are the least effective at getting things done. (Some of the nastiest are also ineffective.)

If we were doing it "right," what would that look like? You can certainly think of things to get rid of — such as endless meetings that never go anywhere. But that is different from having a specific vision of what we could do instead. How would we set the agenda for a better meeting? What would we be talking about? Who would make decisions about who does what? It will be hard to get rid of bad practices unless we have a vision of better ones to replace them.

As you clarify your vision of working well together, you do not want to put yourself above your fellow workers. As an equal, you are trying to improve the level of cooperation.

We Don't Know How to Influence Others' Behavior

If you knew how to organize your own work and had a clear vision of the cooperation you would like to see, there would still be a problem. It is likely that you lack techniques for getting others to adopt better behavior.

We have seen people in charge — people who have all the authority they could want — try with little success to make things work. Bad habits are developed over a lifetime. They don't change at a word. Orders will not give anyone new skills. Most executives have learned that explicit instructions to refrain from engaging in "turf battles" do not stop jockeying for jurisdiction. And for good reason. If one employee unilaterally stopped defending her turf, she could expect to have less and less turf to defend.

If those with full authority find it difficult to improve the quality of collaboration among their subordinates, how can you — one of those subordinates — expect to change the behavior of your fellow workers?

Having no particular expertise in working efficiently alone, no clear vision of the "working-together practices" that you would like a group to adopt, and no strategy for bringing about such collaboration, you have three good reasons for doing nothing.

Besides, doing nothing is a lot easier.

PRESCRIPTION: BUILD PERSONAL SKILLS, CLARIFY GOALS, THEN INFLUENCE OTHERS

Fixing a fractured group often seems hopeless. Coordinating people with different habits is so hard that we often assume there is not much that one person can do. Yet, in practice, some groups do work together better than others. It can't simply be luck. They must be doing something differently.

Thinking further, there are some people who make a difference. We all know an individual who, without authority to tell others what to do, produces order out of chaos. When she or he is one of the group, there are fewer arguments, more focus, more energy, and better harmony — and more gets done. In some offices it is a semiretired veteran executive. In others it is a secretary. How does one person do that? If you want to be such a person, how do you do it?

This book lays out simple guidelines for you to become someone like that. Its purpose is to equip you, the reader, with tools and strategies: for building personal skills, for clarifying a vision of better collaboration, and for nudging colleagues toward that vision.

First, Enhance Your Ability to Contribute by Improving Your Personal Skills

The easiest conduct to change is your own. You empower others by first empowering yourself. Your ability to help others get things done will be greater if you have a systematic way of getting things done by yourself. You start by improving your own personal skills.

Back to the jazz group. Imagine that you are a member of the band. You want it to sound better. Part of getting the band to sound better is becoming a skillful player yourself. Beyond practice, it will help to learn some organizing concepts that are relevant to playing any music and any musical instrument. These might be rhythm, scales, melody, and chords. Learning how to "lead" fellow musicians is not simply learning the techniques of a conductor, say tapping a music stand with a baton and waving one's arms appropriately in the air. Whether you are a designated leader or simply a fellow member of a jazz group, you will want to develop the personal skill of playing music well, and understanding some basic elements that are helpful to you and to others. And as you become a good lateral leader of the band, you will also want to become a good follower.

Consider a medical doctor, who diagnoses and deals with illness by organizing his knowledge into relevant categories (the digestive system, the blood system, the nervous system, the skeletal system, and so on). Such categories are powerful aids to understanding, to spreading knowledge, and to getting things done.

As teachers, we have found that in order to improve the way people negotiate with each other it is extremely helpful to have a handful of basic elements in mind — interests, options, criteria, communication, relationship, commitment, and alternatives to negotiation — elements that are relevant to every negotiation and any culture. Similarly, in workshops focused on helping people learn to work together, participants have found it useful to have a small number of basic elements into which they can group lessons that seem important. The most useful theory for practitioners is neither a complex analysis of everything involved nor a detailed set of "dos and don'ts." Rather it is a handful of organizing elements, few enough to remember and important enough to be useful.

In this book we suggest five basic elements that are highly relevant to getting things done, whether working alone or with others. Each has a chapter devoted to it:

Purpose (Chapter Three).

It is hard to do anything well unless you are clear on what you are trying to do. Some purposes energize and inspire, help measure progress, and help make decisions. Other purposes don't. And people who have the chance to influence the purpose will work harder toward it.

Thinking (Chapter Four).

All of us tend to slip into aimless and haphazard thinking. A few simple techniques can make your thinking more disciplined and focused — can help you generate new ideas and turn them into operational plans. When people work together those same techniques for thinking can convert extra heads around a table from a burden into an asset.

LEARNING (Chapter Five).

No amount of thinking can guarantee a good solution to a problem. You need to test your ideas by experimenting in the real world. Together with others you can adopt a few *learning* habits that help improve your *working* habits.

ENGAGEMENT (Chapter Six).

People can work with enthusiasm or disinterest. The challenges you set for yourself influence your personal level of engagement. The same applies to a group. Instead of accepting a low level of involvement as given, you can increase it by allocating tasks that stimulate commitment, and by the *way* in which you allocate them.

FEEDBACK (Chapter Seven).

One strategy for learning is to experiment in the real world to test your thinking by observing the results. Another is to profit from a colleague's observations and advice. You can get better at giving advice and at receiving it. You can spread those skills to colleagues. Your organization can become one in which feedback is sought and offered in a supportive, rather than a competitive, spirit.

You will first want to develop a personal skill in dealing with each of those five elements, whether your task is to "make music" by yourself, or to influence a group to "make better music" together. In either situation you will want to be clear on your purpose, to think systematically, and so on.

Second, Clarify a Vision of Good Collaboration As Jointly Using the Same Five Skills

Again, consider our analogy to a jazz group. You want to know how to play music yourself, *and* you want to have a clear idea of what "playing good jazz together" sounds like.

The basic elements of rhythm, notes, scales, melody, and chords provide a useful structure for thinking about how to improve both your personal skills and the way your group plays jazz together. Whether you are leading informally as a fellow player or you are an official "conductor" leading a symphony orchestra, you will want to have a clear idea of successful collaboration. You will want to understand the goal you are trying to help bring about. Before you set out to improve how you and your office mates work together, you will want to have a vision of what that looks (or sounds) like.

Chapters Three to Seven not only explain the basic elements and corresponding skills that will help you as an individual get jobs done; they also describe the joint use of those same five skills as a goal. Having understood some basic organizing elements of getting things done by yourself, you can use those same organizing elements to understand the task of getting things done together.

Then Learn Some Basic Techniques for Stimulating Good Conduct in Others

The skills you learn to get things done efficiently by yourself illuminate the goal of effective collaboration when you are working with others. They will also enhance your personal ability to help bring it about. A clear purpose — in the form of a series of realistic goals — will keep you on track. With clear systematic thinking you can analyze the current state of your collaboration and decide what changes need to be made. You can use learning techniques to profit from the successes and failures of your initial efforts. You can pick those areas for improvement in your collaboration most likely to motivate and engage you. You can look for feedback from colleagues on the ways you tried to influence them and from ways they may have tried to influence you.

In addition to the five basic elements of getting things

done, you need a simple strategy for influencing others. If you are an equal member of that jazz group playing your own instrument, you will not issue commands to the other players. Instead you will lead laterally. You may play a simple phrase and, by a nod, a smile, or a few words, invite others to "take it away." You will also build on contributions that others make. You will model the kind of collaborative improvisation that you think the group would like to have. Each of us can help stimulate others to make their best efforts in a way that will bring our joint efforts to a high level. Three simple ways to get others working toward better methods are:

- To ASK a question that gets others thinking about a collaborative problem and looking for a solution.
- To OFFER your own thoughts, and invite others to use them, build on them, or correct them.
- To DO something that will serve as a model for better behavior.

SPECIFICALLY, THIS BOOK

Each of the five central chapters, which focuses on one element and a corresponding skill, is divided into these three sections. FIRST, you learn the skill as a way of helping you personally get things done when you are working alone. SECOND, you clarify your goal. You create a vision of what it would be like for all of you in the group to be using that skill together. THEN you go back to using those skills and the basic techniques of ASK, OFFER, and DO to change the way you and your colleagues work together. Whether your goal is a substantive one (such as to build a shed) or a process one (to improve the way you and colleagues work together to build a better shed with less effort) the personal skills you develop will both clarify your goal and help you achieve it.

In this first chapter we offered a brief introduction to the five elements and the corresponding skills. Chapter Two develops the rest of the lateral leadership method, the techniques and tactics of which are illustrated in the balance of the book.

2 LATERAL LEADERSHIP

Chapter One offers an overview of our approach to getting things done. The first step is to identify skills you can develop that will make you more successful at getting results. Second is a clear picture of the way a group would be interacting if everyone used those same skills together. Later chapters will deal with one skill at a time, detailing how you can develop that skill and how you and others can use it together. Yet knowing what you want others to do accomplishes little unless you know how to get them to work with you. Your organization will not change unless colleagues decide to adopt those skills and habits. This chapter examines the problem of stimulating others to change their behavior.

PROBLEM: YOU CAN'T MAKE OTHERS CHANGE

Everyone knows what it is like to sit in a meeting that goes nowhere. You may be familiar with the frustration of coming every morning into an office where colleagues have trouble working together. But what can you do about it?

There are two standard responses to being in a group that has internal problems: lie back and do nothing, or take charge and tell people what they should do. Neither works. If you avoid the problem nothing will change. At best, you won't make matters worse. But whatever is causing the trouble does not go away.

Trying to set others straight doesn't go well, either. You may have seen someone else try to improve the way we work together, have little success, and get treated badly for her pains. Sometimes a helpful suggestion is abruptly dismissed: "Don't waste our time. We have work to do." Sometimes the one who makes a suggestion is criticized: "Who do you think you are, my boss?" In the face of such results, it is tempting to shrug your shoulders and say, "Well, what can I do?"

You can also respond by asking seriously, "What *can* I do?" After all, the situation is not hopeless. We have all seen some groups that work well together. You have probably worked in groups that got more done than others. You can likely think of people who are good at fostering collaboration — people who make a team work better. Think of the people in your office that you would want assigned to a project you were working on.

There's a chance you can figure out what these people are doing that works. If so, you can do it yourself. The authors have tried to figure it out and in this chapter suggest some answers. You can check the reasoning and adopt it, or you may be able to do better.

Finding answers to the question, "What can I do?" starts with understanding why attempts to change the way people work together so often fail. It is easy to see why doing nothing fails to improve a situation. But why does giving good instruction to a colleague work so poorly?

DIAGNOSIS: *TELLING* DOES NOT INSPIRE OTHERS TO LEARN NEW BEHAVIOR

One diagnosis is that setbacks in an effort to improve collaboration are the fault of your coworkers. Maybe they are not sophisticated enough to understand the importance of looking at how the group works together. Maybe a coworker has such a need for control that he cannot stand to see someone else exercising influence. Maybe some people are so cantankerous that they could never get along with others.

Such explanations could well be true. Or they could be wrong. One reason you should be suspicious is that these diagnoses tend to exonerate you. There is a universal human tendency to blame others for problems (and to take credit for successes). You would rather believe that the difficulty of getting others to adopt new behavior is their fault, not your own. Knowing your own bias, you should doubt self-serving explanations.

You have another reason to look further. Ascribing all fault to coworkers is a dead end. If the problem is that you work with bad people, then there is nothing to do except resign yourself to the current situation — or resign your job and go elsewhere. It would be a lucky break for you if at least part of the problem were the result of your behavior. Then you could improve the situation by improving your contribution. The more you contribute to a bad situation, the more power you have to change it. In looking to find your own contribution to problems, don't feel guilty. Rather, focus on your own actions instead of blaming others because that makes it easier to empower yourself.

So, if colleagues don't react the way you want them to, start with the assumption that you are doing something wrong.

Telling Others What to Do Implies They Have Lower Status

All of us are concerned with ourselves. Whatever you say, your words will be heard in terms of what they imply about the listener, and the relationship between you. If the listener does not like the implied message about her, she may reject the substance of your message.

Colleagues hear telling as an accusation. Even a question can be heard as an implicit judgment about the other. A man got up early on Saturday morning, after a hard week at the office. Over breakfast he thought about chores that he might do around the house. He liked manageable tasks that took his mind off the big problems at the office. "Is the basement still a mess?" he asked his wife. "Thanks," she shot back. "You don't do anything to help all week, and then you complain about how messy the basement is. Don't blame me."

On Monday he goes to work as line manager at an assembly plant. Partway through the morning he telephones the purchasing office about some equipment he needs to keep his line running:

LINE MANAGER: When will those electric motors be delivered? You told me they'd be here last Wednesday.

PURCHASING AGENT: That was before you changed the order to get larger motors. When you change the order delivery gets delayed. Everybody knows that.

LINE MANAGER: Well, I didn't think of it. Can't we . . . never mind. Next time tell me so that we won't get confused about this again. When someone changes an order tell them when the new delivery date is.

PURCHASING AGENT: We followed our standard procedure. No one *else* ever had a problem with it. If you got confused that's not my fault.

Sound familiar? In both cases, concern with making improvements is heard as an accusation. The conversation is quickly diverted to an unproductive personal exchange. Why?

Any time you give directions there is a risk that the recipient will hear you to imply: "You are the problem. I have the solution." A colleague is concerned about his self-esteem and his standing. He wants to think of himself as competent and respected by others. He doesn't want to be blamed.

A suggestion for change is easily heard as an accusation. People often assume that there's no need to improve how we are working together unless things go badly. "If it ain't broke, don't fix it." The corollary is that if it needs to be fixed, it must be broken. And, if it is broken, then somebody broke it. Thus, "Maybe we could do things better" becomes "Things are a mess and you are to blame." When you give instructions on improving collaboration it is easy to irritate this sensitivity. Even well-intended remarks can be taken as personal criticism.

When people think they have been attacked, they respond. Some deny that anything is wrong, so that there is no cause for blame. "Oh come on, it's not that bad. Relax." Others attack a suggestion to avoid any criticism for not having adopted it sooner. "That would never work." Still others may attack you for making a suggestion. "Are you telling me how to do my job?"

One response to such behavior is to think, "What a jerk. I was only trying to be helpful," and think less of them. A better response: "Their reaction is natural. Now that I know why they respond that way, I may be able to intervene more skillfully."

Colleagues hear you assigning them lesser roles. A consideration seldom discussed but often in the mind of someone being asked to adopt a new method of doing things is "What role do I get in this new scheme?" She may also ask, "What part do I play in the task of making the change?" A coworker may react badly to any attempt to improve the way we work together if she feels left out of the action. Someone else is making decisions; she is being excluded. She may fear that you are trying to take charge of the group, leaving her to occupy a lesser role.

Imagine that you are at a meeting of the sales staff for your department. Suppose you suggest that instead of simply reciting the sales you made last week, you swap advice about how to pitch the clients you will see this week. If others agree with the suggestion, what story would they tell about it? "Lucy came up with a great idea. We went along with it. She's the one who leads the group. I'm one of the followers." If they oppose your suggestion, they have a different story to tell themselves. "She had some goofy idea, but we didn't let her tell us what to do." If those two stories are the only choices, everyone has a reason to oppose your initiative. Colleagues are less likely to support a proposal that appears to leave them out of any credit for creating it.

Worse, they may accept being shut out. Many people avoid confrontation. If they are left out of the action, they may withdraw entirely and let someone else do the work. If you want a team to have the full benefit of everyone's ideas and energy, inducing people to drop out is not the answer.

Telling Them What to Do Fails to Persuade Them

What you *do* say may be heard as identifying someone else as the problem, and as giving them an inferior role. What you *fail* to say is likely to leave them with no understanding of your reasoning, no participation in the thinking, and no demonstration that the ideas can work.

People don't understand why they should change. A friend of the authors is a management consultant who designs change programs for corporations. Most of his clients are large information technology companies. He says that the biggest mistake management makes is not explaining *why* the company is changing a procedure. Employees know the cost and hassle of changing how they do things, but have no idea why a change will be an improvement. Of course they resist. Or they go through the motions, but compliance is halfhearted. The same may be true of times you have tried to convince colleagues to adopt a new method.

But why don't you share the reasoning behind a proposal? You may not be entirely aware of your own reasoning. A light bulb goes on in your head, you think that it is a good idea, but often you cannot articulate why it is so good, even to yourself. You may be reluctant to expose your reasoning for fear that someone will find a flaw in it. Or you may not have the vocabulary to talk about it. How we work together is a complex subject. You probably know a lot about what works and what doesn't, but may not have a tidy explanation of why. It is tempting to say, "Look, just go along with my plan. Trust me."

They have not participated in your thinking. Even if you explain your thinking process with great clarity, the plan remains yours, not theirs. They have no "ownership" of the ideas that you tell them to implement. Someone who has had no opportunity to participate in the thinking and to contribute to the result is likely to have little enthusiasm for carrying it out.

They have not seen your ideas in action. A suggestion to do something is often wholly unpersuasive if it stays at the theoretical level of ideas and words. We have often been told that "actions speak louder than words" — but too often that adage remains mere words. A failure to practice what you preach will undercut anything you say. Your demonstration of inaction provides an excellent excuse for not doing what you tell others to do.

PRESCRIPTION: LEAD LATERALLY TO AVOID THE NEGATIVE CONSEQUENCES OF TELLING OTHERS WHAT TO DO

If telling others what to do is so often ineffective, what should you do instead? In essence, the lateral leadership method invites colleagues to work with you to solve problems. There is little chance of saving the day single-handedly. Don't try to provide a solution to every problem. The key is to improve the process of working together. Start the habit of everyone working to improve collaborative methods. If you can do that, together the group will produce an endless stream of constructive next steps. In short, solutions are not the answer. The answer is a better process for finding solutions.

To affect the behavior of colleagues you want to provide information, analysis, ideas, and suggestions that come from an equal, not from someone of superior status. You are informally "negotiating" what will be your future joint behavior. As in any negotiation, what you suggest is always open to joint consideration. There is an enormous difference between telling others what they have to do, and inviting them to participate. What you say ought not to be an order, an instruction, or a command, nor is it a definitive judgment about what is right or wrong. At the same time, both questions and suggestions should be sufficiently specific to open a door to activities that are attractive, clear, and manageable.

Others are more likely to help you change the way you work together if they feel they get something out of it. Of course, down the road everyone will benefit if you all improve your practices. In addition, it helps to offer colleagues something right now, participation in making something better and in deciding how we do it. By questions and suggestions, the work can be made attractive for them — like Tom Sawyer getting his friends to paint the fence. Whether Tom bamboozled his friends or met their interests in finding something to do, you need not trick your colleagues. Helping improve collaboration is certainly as rewarding as painting a fence. To avoid the negative reactions that so often occur if you tell a colleague to do something, look for specific steps that fall within the broad scope of asking questions, offering suggestions, or doing something yourself that models the sort of behavior you would like to stimulate.

Separate the Person from the Problem

Make it safe to talk about problems in your collaboration. Try to convince your colleagues that looking at what is going wrong is no threat — that you are not trying to blame them.

Blame joint methods, not your colleagues. It will be easier for colleagues to join you in improving the process if they are not worried about being criticized. That should not be difficult. After all, the goal is not to blame someone for a problem, but to improve things. A good approach is to sit side by side, facing a difficulty together. You jointly look for *what* is the cause of a problem, not *who*. As you talk, it should become clear that any confrontation is with the problem, not between you and a colleague.

By definition, interaction is something that you create together. No one person can be wholly responsible for problems that arise in that interaction. And no one is entirely free from responsibility, either. Instead of looking at personal virtue or fault, ask about the methods you are using, and if they are the most efficient ones available. The question is not whether a colleague is a good carpenter or a bad one, but whether you are using hammers when a saw would be better.

Recall the line manager who didn't get his electric motors on time. He might tell the purchasing agent, "You'll have to do better than that or we'll both go talk with our supervisor about your unhelpful attitude." While possibly justified, the immediate effect is to make the purchasing agent defensive, and press him to think of reasons that any problem is someone else's fault. He will look for reasons that he couldn't do things any other way. Placing the blame on the joint interaction gives him different incentives. "It seems like this turned out badly. I didn't ask if the date would change, and I don't recall your telling me. We both assumed there would be no problem. Perhaps we could adopt a different approach. Can you think of something that would help?"

Acknowledge good reasons for another's behavior. When colleagues act in ways that seem unproductive, they likely do so for a reason. Few people have the goal of preventing you from getting more done. More likely, they are responding rationally to a perceived interest. Someone may be abrupt because he faces an important deadline and wants to get back to work. Another may disparage an attempt to be creative because she has high standards, and wants to keep looking for an even better idea. There might be more constructive ways for them to pursue such goals — but the goals are typically legitimate. Try to imagine what a good motivation for their behavior might be. When you discuss an issue, start with the assumption that they would like to help. "I know you have been terribly busy and perhaps concerned about cutting costs. Still I would welcome your thinking on an issue that has been on my mind . . . "

Knowing that you want to see their point of view will make it easier for them to see yours. And it will reassure them that you appreciate their concerns, and that any new proposal will take their concerns into account.

Accept a share of responsibility. The degree of successful collaboration in a group is the sum of individual behavior. Everyone contributes to the difficulties. You may not be aware of how you are contributing to unhelpful dynamics. Your colleagues almost certainly are.

It would be wise to take on responsibility for some share of the problem. "I think we could make this team work better. I'm sure that I have been contributing as much as anyone to the difficulties we've been having. Let's try to figure out how we could run a tighter ship." In talking about mistakes you may have made, being specific makes you more convincing. You don't want to say, "Okay, so I'm not perfect." Instead, say something more like: "I'm afraid we have been talking past each other. Certainly I have. Linda was explaining her idea when I interrupted and started talking about mine. That wasn't helpful. Maybe we could list a number of ideas, and then discuss them one at a time. Let's start with Linda's."

Taking a share of the responsibility for the current situation is accurate. And it will make others less defensive. It shows that it is safe to admit that one's behavior can be improved, and that you are not out to get anyone.

Think About Roles As Others May See Them

By asking questions and offering suggestions you help shape a role for another. Trying to improve the way a group works together is a little like making a movie. When colleagues are deciding whether to accept a role, the big question in each mind is likely to be, "Do I get a good part?" You want to help create roles that both satisfy your colleagues and help the group be productive and efficient.

Make it attractive. You will not be able to change the way a group works without getting everyone — or nearly everyone — to take part. The way to do that is by helping design a role that each person will want to play. The role should be active. Few will want to sit on the sidelines watching others perform. A role will be inviting to the extent that it gives the person something interesting to do. Second, the role should be one that commands respect — self-respect and respect from others.

No one is likely to leap at an offer if it sounds like, "Why don't you do the dishes while the rest of us plan for tomorrow's picnic." A role will be more attractive to the extent that it lets others use and demonstrate their abilities. Most people are not too concerned about being elevated above their peers, but few like to be treated as inferior.

Make it empowering. You will get more recruits if you suggest roles that empower your coworkers. Most of us want to feel that we are able to make a difference. People will more gladly take part in an enterprise if they have some measure of control over what they do and where the group is going.

If colleagues get the chance to improve their skills everyone will benefit. More important, they will get in the habit of making a difference. Even if you are the only one in the group who is now exercising lateral leadership to improve the way you work together, you will be better off. If others are also using their initiative, their ideas, and their energy to improve the way you work together, better still. The successful use of lateral leadership skills will be demonstrated when those with whom you are working become equally or more skillful.

Involve Colleagues in Planning Changes

If a change in our methods is to be effective, everyone on the team needs to understand it, and try to make it work. The best way to achieve both of these goals is to give everyone a hand in shaping the change. Everyone will know why this idea was chosen, and everyone will feel sufficient ownership of the new practice to want it to succeed.

Keep an Open Mind

You will want colleagues to be open to your ideas. The best way to encourage an open mind in others is to have one yourself. And it will be a lot easier to convince colleagues that you are open to their point of view if it is true. The goal is not to have others listen to your thinking and agree with every word. You want to get the benefit of your colleagues' thinking. Every idea can be improved. The authors think that the guidelines for improving the way people work together spelled out in this book are excellent. *And* we have no doubt that they can be improved. If we worked on them for another year they would probably get better. With questions and suggestions from readers, they will definitely improve. But we could never make them perfect for any one reader. Every reader can tailor these ideas in different ways.

And if you propose one of the practices suggested in this book, a colleague could improve it. Don't become too attached to your first proposal (or to a later one). Listen to coworkers, and be eager to adopt the best of their thinking.

If someone else is trying to improve collaboration, support her. Don't try to top her idea or focus attention on another issue. You will get a chance later. The worst meetings are those composed entirely of professional mediators and facilitators — each one struggles to prove that he knows the most about improving how people cooperate. Part of being a good leader is knowing when to be a good follower.

PUTTING IT INTO PRACTICE: CHOOSE A TACTIC FOR INVITING THEM TO THINK ALONG

The general prescriptions in this chapter can be turned into simple, operational tactics for encouraging others to contribute. If telling others what to do doesn't work, three methods that will cause less resistance are: ASK a question, OFFER an idea, and DO something that will serve as a model for replication. These techniques are not tricks or phony devices. Success in using them depends on honesty. When you are curious and interested in an answer, you ask honest questions.

(Asking "Why are you such an idiot?" is not an honest question.) You will want to offer ideas that you recognize to be just that — ideas. They are not conclusions, decisions, or announcements, but rather possibilities open for discussion and reexamination. And when you do something, it should be something useful. It should serve as an example of someone's taking a constructive initiative, not of someone's putting on a performance merely for show. This principle of transparent honesty suggests a few guidelines.

ASK Them to Contribute Their Thoughts

The easiest way to enlist others in changing joint work habits is to ask questions. It focuses attention on an issue without asserting one answer that a colleague may resist. Done properly, it doesn't put anyone on the spot. Most people like to be seen to be helping aim a group's efforts. Few object to being asked for advice, as long as they are not being interrogated.

Explain the purpose of a question. Even a genuine, open question can make someone anxious if they wonder why you are asking it. Recall the husband who asked if the basement was still messy — to determine whether he should spend the morning cleaning it out. His wife attributed another intention — that he was "asking" as an indirect form of criticizing her for not cleaning it.

If colleagues do not understand why you are asking, they may suspect the worst. It is better if they can concentrate on the question instead of wondering what you are implying. Taking a moment to explain your purpose can ease the recipient's mind. "M'love, I am thinking about what chores I might do today. What do *you* think needs to be done? The basement?" Similarly, you are likely to get a more helpful response from the supplier if you say something like "Joe, I need your help. I know we changed the specification for those motors, but we do need them urgently. Without them, the line will slow down and I'll hear about it from my boss. Is there anything I can do that will make it easier for you to get them to us?"

Ask real questions. It is easy to fall into the habit of using a question to push an agenda on someone else: "We really need to meet at eight tomorrow morning, don't you think?" "Would you agree that the current state of affairs is unacceptable?" While phrased as questions, these statements are really a mechanism to press someone to agree.

Rather than ask leading questions that point to one particular answer, it is better to lead with open questions that point to an area of concern. "What do you think might be causing the problem?" is an open question. Closed questions that are to be answered with a "yes" or a "no" limit participation. "Do you think that Andrew's resistance is causing the problem?" is not an open question. Encourage coworkers to be full and equal participants.

Colleagues can usually tell if you already have an answer in mind when you ask a question. Instead of thinking afresh, they will guess what your view is. Whether they agree with that view or refute it is likely to depend as much on how they feel about you as on a fresh consideration of the question. They may also resent your asking leading questions, as though you were a school teacher and they were pupils.

OFFER Your Thoughts

What if you *do* have a view? There is no need to pretend to ask a question when you think you already know a good answer. When you have information, ideas, suggestions, and opinions, it is fine to share them.

In ordinary parlance, there is no difference between *telling* someone your thoughts and *offering* your thoughts. For the purpose of this discussion, the distinction is between telling others that they should adopt your thinking, and offering it for their consideration. Telling is like issuing commands: "This is what we have to do." Offering ideas is exploratory: "This is one thing we could do, if we can't think of something better." Like a good host, you can leave an idea out for a colleague to take if she chooses. Do not thrust it on her. You want to be looking for the best idea from whatever source, not advocating one idea. Encourage disagreement on the merits. Let others decide whether to use your idea as a starting point, discard it, or adopt it.

Offering ideas should encourage others to join in the thinking. Instead of shutting them out, it draws them in. It invites them to be a judge of ideas and an inventor of new ones.

Contribute one piece of the puzzle. Improving collaboration can be a little like doing a crossword puzzle together. It isn't a good outcome for you — or anyone else — to be working on it alone, while everyone else waits or strains to look over your shoulder. You will get a better solution, more involvement, and less resentment if you pass the puzzle around.

You may well have a good idea. But it isn't sacrosanct. It isn't a painting by Rembrandt, which could only be marred by further work. Better if you make a few strokes and then pass the brush to someone else. Encourage others to sharpen any idea, and to improve on it. Invite them to move the thinking forward. "The way we're writing this proposal doesn't seem to be working. I have been revising your version, then you look at my draft and put some of the same things back in. I think it is because I haven't understood the thinking behind your writing and perhaps you haven't understood mine. Does that sound right? What do you think we might do about it?" You can encourage others to invent detailed plans for implementing an idea. "I think we need to understand each other's reasoning about a change before switching it back. How should we do that? We could put in a footnote explaining the reasoning, or we might read it aloud and discuss it. Do you have an idea?"

The four-quadrant approach developed in Chapter Four makes it easy to offer some data, analysis, or fresh ideas in one quadrant, and then ask for further thinking that builds on it. You can share some observations about the way things are working, and then invite others to share their observations, or to suggest a diagnosis that explains them.

Invite others to challenge your thinking. Some may be reluctant to dispute your analysis, for fear of provoking a dispute. Others, not sure how to argue with an idea, may confront you personally. In either case the smart play is to make it easy for others to challenge your thinking rather than you. Disclosing the steps of your reasoning helps others test your conclusions. The more explicit you can make your mental process, the easier it will be to find and correct flaws. There will be less danger that "groupthink" will produce a foolish plan, and less risk of friction among team members.

DO Something Constructive

By taking action you can influence others' behavior in either of two ways. Action is sometimes the best way to explain an idea. Talking about the way we work together can be abstract and confusing. Lengthy attempts at verbal clarification often lead to further confusion and frustration. Most of us are not used to talking about the subject. A picture may be worth a thousand words.

If successful, you will also have demonstrated that someone without the authority to tell others what to do can take an initiative. Directly modeling that behavior, whatever the substance of your action, can send a strong message that we are in this together.

For modeling to send a message, it has to be observed. On his way home late one night, the CEO of a successful cable television company noticed that the carpet in front of the elevator was worn through and torn so that it could easily trip someone. He was disappointed that no one had taken the initiative to fix it. He wished that he had the kind of company where anyone who saw a problem would work on it, instead of wondering whose job description it fell under. The next day he brought some duct tape from his home and in the evening taped over the torn carpet. A few months later the tape came loose. After a week he wondered why again he had to be the one to fix it. Then he realized that no one would follow his example if they never saw him. The next morning at 8:45, some employees found him on his hands and knees patching the rug. In response to their insistence, he allowed them to finish the job.

Modeling behavior will be more visible if it cuts against people's expectations. A senior executive sets a powerful example by picking up coffee cups left at the end of a meeting. His secretary can change expectations about initiative and responsibility by suggesting that department heads may want to get together to exchange information about a current project. No one might pay attention if the two did the opposite tasks. Your attempt to influence others' behavior by example will be most effective when colleagues notice it.

Use the Four Quadrants to Organize and Explain Your Reasoning

When offering your ideas or asking for others, it helps to have a simple structure for thinking about a problem. Conclusions will be more persuasive if you can explain your reasoning simply. And with a little set of standard questions you are never at a loss for ways to invite others to participate in the thinking and to improve upon it. One framework (developed more fully in Chapter Four), which has a proven track record and is easy to use, is the following:

I. Data	II. Diagnosis	III. Direction	IV. Do Next
What is the problem?	What are possible causes?	What strategies might be wise?	What are some specific next steps?

These four quadrants provide a basic way to structure thinking about a problem. When you try to do anything, whether it is a specific job (catching a fish) or improving the way you collaborate (the way you fish together), you can sort thinking into these four categories. It helps divide a complex tangle of issues into discrete units. You can then invite a colleague to take on a manageable piece of the larger task. You can work your way through it step by step, without getting lost in the complexities. With the four-quadrant tool you can assess where a group is in grappling with the problem of collaboration. You can lay the quadrants out in front of the group on flip charts or just ask questions to guide the way.

Assume that several of you who work in different departments of a large corporation have been asked to produce a training schedule for the coming year. The current schedule has received much criticism. You hope that you can produce something better. Unfortunately, at the first of several meetings you see that your collaboration is not going as well as one would hope.

There are two problems. One is the particular problem about WHAT you are trying to do — produce next year's training schedule. The other is the problem about HOW you are working together — your ways of working and interacting with one another. Start on this second problem. If you are going to be effective in jointly designing next year's training program you will want to have the way you work together in good shape.

Perhaps you are so lost in the substantive work that you don't recognize that the difficulty is partly due to your collaborative method. Rather than jumping right to suggestions, call attention to the problem by inviting a discussion about what is actually happening, the DATA.

"Designing a new schedule shouldn't be this hard. I know that we are all busy and need to get back to work. Still, we've been here for forty-five minutes without making much headway. What's happening?"

It may be that everyone knows that the group process is off kilter, and knows pretty clearly what symptoms they don't like. If so, you can try to get people focused on causes — what DIAGNOSIS explains your difficulty. You can examine a number of diagnoses to see which fits the facts most accurately. You can encourage everyone to take a hand in the thinking: "Maybe we are having trouble because we haven't clarified exactly what it is we are trying to achieve here." It turns out that one person thinks you were assigned to produce a report making recommendations for the future; another thinks you should design new courses; a third thinks that you ought to limit yourselves to collecting everyone's complaints and reporting them.

Once everyone agrees on the causes of your difficulty, you can ask a question that moves you along to consider different approaches that might solve it — what DIRECTION you could take. "It might help to clarify our purpose. What do people think should be the product of this committee?"

Often, the piece of the puzzle that is missing is making a good idea operational. If that is the case, you will do the team a service by leading them to focus on a specific step that someone could DO NEXT to make your collaboration better.

"How should we go about clarifying our purpose? What do people think we should have in hand one month from today."

This chapter has described why "telling" is likely to be ineffective and how to apply the lateral leadership method in ways that overcome the difficulties of telling others what to do. The central idea of the strategy is to intervene in a way that will make colleagues feel better about themselves. Instead of feeling criticized, a coworker may feel flattered that she is being asked for her opinion. Instead of resisting a prescribed solution, she will get the chance to work out the reasoning herself and come up with her own ideas. Instead of being put in a subordinate or marginal role, she will be cast as a coleader who could make an important contribution.

The next five chapters each consider in some detail one element of getting things done. Each looks at how to sharpen your personal skill in that element. It then sketches the goal of using that same skill and those practices jointly, and suggests ways in which the lateral leadership techniques of ASK, OFFER, and DO can help bring that about.

PART B.
BASIC ELEMENTS
OF GETTING
THINGS DONE

The previous chapter offers techniques for persuading others to change their behavior. But change it to what? Those techniques won't help much if you don't know what habits and procedures your colleagues should adopt.

Luckily, there is no shortage of advice. Bookstores and magazines are filled with an endless laundry list of ideas: some good, some not. But no one can even read them all. The most useful advice would be simple enough to remember and robust enough to cover most of the problems that arise when we work together.

When doctors study the body, they could be overwhelmed if they tried to learn one list of the thousands of bones and glands and veins. Instead, they simplify the study of anatomy by organizing the body into a few systems — the bone system, the blood system, the nervous system, the digestive system, and so on. This part of the book breaks the problem of group collaboration into a few basic elements. It offers simple advice for handling each element in your personal work and a snap-shot of what better management of that element in a group would look like.

Lastly, it shows lateral leadership techniques you can use to get others to adopt better habits.

3 PURPOSE

AIM BY FORMULATING RESULTS TO BE ACHIEVED

It is hard to be successful if you don't know what you are trying to achieve. Our first element, PURPOSE, is a good place to start looking at the way your organization works. And before you start analyzing the behavior of others, take a good look at yourself. Do you have the sort of purpose that helps you work productively? If you don't have one now, do you know how to get one?

A young lawyer had just made partner at a prominent New York law firm. Late each night when he left to catch the train, he looked at the firm's mission statement posted in the lobby. It read:

> Our mission is to achieve a high degree of excellence in legal practice, to zealously serve our clients, and to provide professional and personal satisfaction for our attorneys and staff.

The statement stuck in his head, and he thought about it on the train ride home. "A high degree of excellence in legal practice," he mused. "I don't even know what that is. I have no idea how I could tell when I got there, or why I should work hard to do so, or, if so, what I should do about it tomorrow."

FIRST, DEVELOP A PERSONAL SKILL: SHARPEN YOUR PURPOSE

Before you can improve the way a group sets a purpose, you need to develop skill in formulating your own purpose. Skill in aiming your efforts means having some standard practices that help do it — even when you are working alone. Start developing those practices by taking a hard look at your current habits about choosing goals.

PROBLEM: EVEN WHEN YOU WORK HARD, THERE IS OFTEN LITTLE TO SHOW FOR IT

There have probably been times when you were in the middle of doing something and suddenly asked yourself, "Why am I doing this?" Or you find yourself jumping from one activity to another. You react to a phone call, to a letter, or to a colleague who walks in. And you are in good company. A study of executives in large organizations found that a substantial proportion of their time was spent being interrupted by colleagues — or interrupting them. Most of us spend time on things that have little or no relationship to what we would like to accomplish. Sometimes the harder we work, the less we get done.

CAUSE: YOU LACK A USEFUL PURPOSE

One explanation of that difficulty is that you lack a useful understanding of the purpose of your work. Like our young lawyer, you may have some official reason for what you are doing. Yet it isn't a purpose that helps you get things done.

Lacking purpose hurts performance. The Book of Proverbs says "Where there is no vision, the people perish." If you have no purpose in mind, it is hard to know whether you are doing a good job. Even if instructions are precise, not knowing *why* you are doing something will dampen your motivation. Who wants to work on a task that has no point? In the army not so long ago a form of discipline was to make an errant soldier dig a deep hole and fill it back up. For a soldier accustomed to hard work, the worst part of the exercise was its futility. Working without a purpose is punishment.

The conventional wisdom in management theory is that articulating a mission is vital to improving performance. Everyone knows that. And the conventional wisdom is right. But then, why don't you regularly articulate your mission — your purpose? What explains your actual behavior? Consider some possible diagnoses.

You React to the Past Instead of Shaping the Future

One explanation may be that we tend to look back more naturally than forward. The word "why?" can ask two quite different questions:

- "What *caused* me to do something?"
- "For what *purpose* am I doing it?"

The first question looks back for an antecedent event. The second question looks forward to a desired result.

We all frequently fail to distinguish between the stimulus

that caused us to act and the purpose or goal that we want to bring about. Too often when asked to explain our actions we respond with a sentence that begins, "Because . . ." and refers to some past event, rather than with a sentence that begins, "In order to . . ." and points to the future.

Antecedent events do provide a good reason for acting. Perhaps most of our actions are stimulated by prior events, whether it be mounting costs, running out of storage space, a fight, a famine, or a flood. When the triggering event is a request from someone else, we often fail to consider our purpose adequately. It's easier to leave the thinking to a superior, and carry out a limited set of instructions, than to take responsibility for accomplishing a goal.

Yet even when acting on instructions from a superior, an antecedent cause is not enough.

"Why are you getting a newspaper in such a hurry?"

"Because my boss told me to."

Such instructions from a boss are a good enough reason to go after a newspaper. Presumably you don't want to ignore or disobey them. On the other hand, you will likely do a better job if you know for what purpose the paper is wanted. Does your boss want paper to put under a can of dripping paint? Or does she want the latest news on Bosnia, or the current price of the company's stock?

If you don't know the purpose then you don't know whether to get an old newspaper out of a stack in the closet, to buy today's paper from the newsstand, or to check the stock price on the Internet. Without understanding a goal, your actions are unlikely to be well chosen.

We often avoid aiming because it is hard work. Looking forward is more difficult than looking back. We know what we have done. It has been said that "hindsight is an exact science." Describing what we will be trying to achieve requires an effort of imagination. In part, the problem stems from the way our minds perceive reality. The events of the past are real, immediate, vivid. The future for which we plan is uncertain, vague, shadowy. It takes effort to focus our minds on the future rather than on things that are affecting us now.

You Have a Purpose, But It Doesn't Help

Deciding to adopt a forward-looking purpose is only the first step. Just as we sometimes work blindly because we look back to a stimulus rather than forward to the purpose, the same can be true of aiming itself.

You know that a company or a government agency is supposed to have a mission statement. Everybody says so. Stockholders and officials expect it. People are far less clear on why they should have one. Unless you look forward to the purpose for which you want a purpose, your aiming may still be ineffective. As a result, many organizations have mission statements or goals that do not serve to motivate their employees, direct their efforts, or help them make decisions about priorities.

Most mission statements suffer from one or more of several flaws.

It fails to inspire. Some clearly articulated purposes do not motivate. This is particularly true when a task is routine: File the data so that we know where to get it if we ever need it; fill out the forms so the boss can't complain that we have no record. Having a purpose that nobody cares about is almost like having no purpose.

It does not help judge success. Another function served by a well-formulated statement of purpose is to provide some criterion by which we can measures success. At the end of a day, a week, a month, or a year we would like to be able to look back and see that something has been accomplished. We would like to reach a milepost.

It offers no immediate direction. It is possible to have an inspiring vision but no immediate objective. The sort of grand purpose that would inspire you may be so distant that you do not know what to do tomorrow to start achieving it. Consider a nonprofit organization staffed by idealistic people horrified by the human costs of war. They decide that their purpose is "to work for peace." However desirable and laudable peace may be — however inspiring — peace is an insufficient guide for their efforts. They can find themselves proceeding in different directions and even working at cross purposes. One may work for "peace through strength" by supporting government investment in weapons for deterrence. Another may work for peace through disarmament.

Without a statement of purpose that meets these criteria you will find that much of your work is unrelated to any purpose. Roger made a habit of asking students in his legal profession class what, if they should live a full seventy years, would they like a friend to be able to say at a memorial service? The visions were remarkably similar: "Always available to family and friends . . . dedicated to public service . . . helped the community . . . led a balanced life . . ." and so on. When the young workaholics were then asked how the jobs they were seeking or the work they would do as associates were related to achieving that vision, they were dumbstruck by the gap. Distant visions and hard work are both required, but unless what you do today is related to where you want to end up, you will never get there.

It Is Not Easy to Formulate a Purpose

Formulating a purpose that nicely aims your efforts is difficult because of the tension between short- and long-term planning. Looking to the distant future, we can be idealistic, imaginative, and visionary. In the long run, all things may be possible, and we are not limited by concerns of the moment.

Yet big visionary ideas have little impact on what to do today. Too often the day-to-day tasks that keep us busy are unrelated to that distant vision. You work hard, answering questions, phone calls, and letters. You stay busy moving things from an in box into an out box. Yet even thinking about an inspiring long-term vision — when you find time to do so — will not bring it about. No one cares about a purpose that is too small. Yet it may seem as though a big vision could never be accomplished. It may be so far off that it is unclear what could bring it nearer.

APPROACH: FORMULATE A PURPOSE THAT MOTIVATES AND GUIDES YOU

Whatever you are doing, you need to check that you are clear on your purpose. This is true whether you are putting up a fence, writing a report, or trying to improve collaboration with others. It is especially true when your task is choosing a purpose. You want to be clear on why you want one.

Don't Just React, Look Ahead

We often assume that purposes are given, that they preexist, that we have them somewhere. We tend to believe that we can find a purpose simply by scanning our brains to discover what it is. No. A purpose that will be useful will not be found. It has to be worked out.

You do not have to choose between looking back to a cause and looking forward to a goal. You can do both. Looking back to a stimulus may help identify some possible purposes. Looking back can help you understand what should be done, its urgency, and the risk of doing nothing. It will not, however, give sufficient focus to guide your actions. No matter how urgent the stimulus, the only thing that you can affect is the future.

You take a management course "because" your boss recommended it, or "because" the company is paying for it. You may be studying the products of a competitor "because" you were told to. No matter how powerful the stimulus, you will benefit by looking forward and asking yourself to set a purpose.

If you are taking a management course, it is *in order to* accomplish what? What analytical techniques do you want to learn? What skills do you want to acquire? If a group of you are examining a competitor's products, *to what end?* Are you seeking to identify defects and weaknesses that you can point out to your customers? Are you looking for bright ideas from which your company can benefit?

There is always a tension between limiting yourself to steps necessary to achieve a goal and doing other desirable things. Not every activity in every business can be devoted to achieving a particular well-defined long-term vision. Yet there is a serious risk that too much valuable time and energy will be absorbed in reading reports, writing letters of recommendation, welcoming foreign visitors, and otherwise doing "good things" that fail to move you toward the place where you want to be. Every second of your life won't be perfectly aimed at achieving your goals. But the more the better. One of your goals may well be to reduce time devoted to tangential activities. As a manager attending one of Alan's workshops remarked, "The time we have is finite, but the work we *could* do is infinite."

Formulate a Purpose That Will Help Get Things Done

Once you recognize that a purpose — whether for a day, a year, or a lifetime — is something that you choose, you face that choice. All purposes are not equally useful. Some are better than others at helping you be more productive.

What is the purpose for having a purpose? What criteria or standards ought a well-selected purpose meet? If we all work better when we have a clear goal, the same applies to the work of forming goals. For some, an adequate purpose might be: "In order to enjoy myself," or, particularly if you are feeling under a lot of pressure, "In order to get through the day." You will get more done if you are more ambitious. Presumably you are reading this book because you are interested in accomplishing something. A well-crafted set of goals should meet four main criteria:

- To inspire greater efforts.
- To help measure success and evaluate your efforts.
- To engage your efforts today.
- To make sure that each day's work helps accomplish the big results you want to achieve.

Set a Purpose over Three Points in Time

It is not easy to see how the same purpose could fill all the criteria above. If your purpose is grand and inspiring — like ending violence in inner-city schools or launching a startup firm that becomes the leader in its market — then it is hard to see what you could do today that would make that goal happen. If it is a sober, restrained goal that you can accomplish quickly — such as compiling some information for a database on youth crime at one school or looking for ways to meet a potential customer — then it is hard to see that it will make much difference. Caught between choosing a grand purpose or a practical one, the best advice is "don't." Don't choose between them. Identify both. By formulating a statement of purpose in terms of proposed results over three or more points in time you can have:

- An inspiring distant vision.
- A mid-distant goal en route that is a worthy goal in itself.
- Some immediate objectives to start working on at once.

You will want to keep shaping these three targets to make sure that they are "in line."

An inspiring distant vision. You are likely to make the effort necessary to do a good job if your purpose is sufficiently meaningful to enlist some emotional commitment. Clarity is not enough. The task of digging twenty holes in the ground, each six feet deep, and then filling them back up is clear and explicit. It will, however, be a totally unsatisfactory purpose for a day's activities unless you have a good answer to the automatic question, "What for?"

You will want to have a vision of a future situation that will justify the effort. You will want colleagues not merely to conform to expectations — but to contribute voluntarily to a goal they understand. The International Red Cross staff and other relief workers put up with enormous hardships and risks. Their willingness to do so is a function of the nobility of the end. The effort that any of us will devote to a task will depend on whether that task furthers some higher goal. It is easier for us to chip stones all day if we know that we are building a cathedral.

Not every goal will be inspirational. Still, the more clearly a distant vision provides good reason for what you are doing, the better you will work. That purpose may be personal, such as to earn sufficient income to provide a home for your family, or to afford a hiking trip in Alaska. Better still if you can see a purpose related to the job itself, such as to discover where we are wasting money on the production line so that more people can afford the prescription drugs that your company makes. You can make money doing lots of jobs. What is good about this one? It is best if you feel no need to ask, "What is my purpose in doing that?" or to comment, "I can't see any real point in this job." The more self-explanatory the distant goal, the more likely it is to have legitimacy and moral value; and the more likely it is to be meaningful — perhaps inspiring — to those working on a project.

A useful distant goal should be sufficiently remote so that formulating it is not dominated by today's news or immediate concerns. You do not want your planning to be overwhelmed by the limited funds currently in your checking account or by what some member of the board may have said at the last meeting. You want to choose a vision with an eye toward the future, unrestricted by today's preoccupations.

You do not, however, want your vision to be so distant that it will have no impact on what you do now. A goal that is "over the horizon" will not offer a sense of direction. As lofty and inspirational as your vision may be, it should be clear enough and near enough to have some impact on what you do tomorrow.

A mid-term goal to use as a milestone. There was a famous race of small sailing boats off Martha's Vineyard involving a fog, a light breeze, and a strong tide. The boats could see one another but nothing else. With no landmark by which to judge, one crew quietly lowered an anchor to feel which way the boat was moving with respect to the bottom. Finding that they were drifting directly backward, they anchored fast until the tide changed. That boat, which "moved" to the lead as the other boats were pulled back by the tide, eventually won the race.

You will want your purpose to include a basis for gauging how well you are doing. You don't want to wait, perhaps for years, to see whether you accomplish your distant vision. If you measure success only at the end, it will be too late to do anything about it. You will want benchmarks along the way by which to measure progress. A well-formulated statement of purpose should include a mid-distant goal — something realistic and measurable to be accomplished en route to some distant vision. A clearly defined mid-distant goal with a proposed date of achieving it offers a basis for measuring performance while there is still time to make corrections.

As you work toward a long-term vision, there is the possibility that it will remain beyond your reach or that you will decide to veer off toward a different vision. To avoid wasting time, a mid-distant goal should be an accomplishment that is worthwhile whether or not you complete the ultimate vision. Building a bridge halfway across a river would not pass this test. Building a bridge half as wide all the way across the river might.

The division of Kodak that built the Hubble Telescope knew that NASA might stop the project if Congress cut funding for the giant satellite. To avoid wasting their effort, they devoted a team of engineers to making sure that the technology developed for the satellite would have other commercial uses. Where there was a choice between approaches to an engineering problem, they picked the one most likely to be useful in other applications.

Some immediate objectives. An inspiring distant vision offers direction and reasons for doing something. A mid-distant goal offers something measurable and worthwhile to be accomplished en route. There is also a need for immediate activities that will enlist our energies and develop a commitment to the joint project.

There is a high risk that despite all the aiming and all the setting of distant and mid-distant goals, not much will happen unless you answer the question, "What are the next things to be accomplished on the way? What results should we see this week? Each of those goals should take you closer to where you want to be.

Every politician knows that it is not enough to inspire supporters with the distant goal of a better city, clean government,

or a new democracy. Politicians also have immediate activities
to enlist supporters. Potential workers need some immediate
goals to which they can commit. To produce the energetic
commitment that makes political activity effective, candidates
offer their constituents specific things they can start doing
toward immediate goals, such as ring doorbells, stuff
envelopes, lick stamps, distribute posters, respond to mail, or
answer the phones. Once you have started to take action you
are likely to become increasingly committed. Few like to think
they were duped into wasting their efforts. Once you have
worked on a project, you are more likely to consider it important. By starting to do something — particularly something
meaningful toward a distant and lofty goal — you increase the
likelihood that you will shed doubts, put aside ambivalence,
and keep working. (The psychological commitment to keep
believing in what we are doing is so great that we want to
examine our purposes periodically, and check whether they
still seem wise.)

Formulate Your Purpose in Terms of Results to Be Achieved

Goals that sound worthy may fail to provide a sense of direction. One of the primary stated goals of medical doctors is to
"do no harm." That sets an admirable limitation and caution
on their activities, but it fails to give guidance on what to do.
Playing golf, weeding the garden, watching television, and
reading a novel are all ways for a doctor to avoid doing harm.

If you want to get something done instead of merely keeping yourself occupied, your purpose is best framed in terms of
things to be accomplished. The best purpose is not simply that
at various times in the future you will be working hard, or
efficiently, or happily, but that by some future point in time
you will have something in place — something measurable.
You will have built a cathedral, or a barn. You will have
cleared forty acres, or paid off the mortgage. The company

will have a hundred full-time employees, or five. Whatever it is, you should be able to recognize when it has been accomplished.

Briefly stated, good goals are nouns, not adjectives. Wanting to do work that is "excellent" or "world-class" gives no guidance. A small business — say, a landscaping and tree-removal operation with institutional clients — could have a goal of "excellent customer relations." If you are one of the workers dealing with a customer, you will not know what to do. In an excellent relationship is the customer entitled to a discount? When a hurricane knocks trees over, do you serve existing customers first, or rely on the relationship to keep them loyal while you serve new customers? A tangible goal would give better guidance: "One year from now our three largest customers will not put new work out for competitive bids, but will give us the work at our standard price." Then you can think through what you need to do to convince your customers to take that step.

A goal may be a physical product. It might be a report of some kind. In many cases, particularly for people at the top of an organization, it may be changes in behavior of some of its members. The chairman of a large chemical company instituted a major program aimed at getting his managers to have their staff handle technical work instead of doing it themselves. While his long-term objective was to improve performance in manufacturing, he recognized that an interim goal was to bring about a substantial change in the way his managers managed. To be a useful mid-term goal, a change in management style has to be measurable. There are many possible yardsticks. Perhaps the chairman would require the managers to report the name of the competently trained person who will handle each particular technical problem in the future. Or he might require his senior managers to report examples of what they had observed themselves as evidence of changes.

SPECIFIC STEPS: ONE WAY TO
BUILD A SET OF GOALS

There is a well-known story of the stranger who saw a man wandering back and forth under a street light. When the stranger inquired if he could help, the man said he was looking for his car keys, which he had dropped. After looking for some time, the stranger inquired if the man could remember where he had dropped them. The man replied: "About half a block down the street, but the light here is so much better." We do not want to be pursuing next steps simply because they are easy.

If your efforts are to be effective, the different goals you accomplish should reinforce one another rather than cancel one another out. The efforts you make over time should be cumulative, each building on the last. They should be in the same direction, both right now and in the future. This means that your distant vision, your mid-distant goal, and your immediate objectives should be aligned. Together they should serve as a compass that will point out a direction in which to proceed.

The vision of where you would like to go should dominate the means for getting there, both your mid-distant goal and your next steps. Do not take next steps, no matter how simple, that fail to take you in the direction you want to go. Having formed an idea of the kind of goal that would be useful — a set of tangible objectives set across three or more points in time — you can start thinking about how to pick the goals.

Start with the Goal That Inspires Most Confidence

Sometimes you are motivated by a distant vision: "Ten years from now I want our company to have branches all over the globe." Or you may be happy with your day-to-day tasks, confident that they are directed toward good ends. "I am proud of our company. I like what I do." Start with some objective that makes sense, and line up the others with it.

Revise Near and Distant Goals Until They Are Aligned

Wherever you start, work out toward the future and back toward the present until you have formulated and are satisfied with proposed accomplishments at different points in time.

Ask "for what purpose?" Sometimes you have thought little about long-term purposes, but know what you would like to achieve tomorrow. If you have a tentative hypothesis about a next step, ask "why? In order to accomplish what?"

When you have an answer to that question, ask the same question again, and keep repeating until you can go no further. In probing your motives you need not look for the one "right" answer. Better to generate a list of possible purposes from which to choose.

If, for example, you enjoy much of the day-to-day practice of law but not all of it, it might be worthwhile to ask yourself, "For what purpose am I practicing law?" Is there any reason not to quit and do something else? If your reasons are reactive — if you quit you won't know how to pay the mortgage — formulate some positive reasons for practicing law. On reflection, you may find that you prefer to represent some types of clients and not others. Perhaps you like representing less affluent communities in environmental litigation. Maybe you want to help high-tech startups that spur economic growth. Either way, you might tentatively adopt a mid-distant goal of finding a few friends and jointly setting up your own firm where you could devote more time to particular types of clients.

Then you have to ask yourself the same question again, "What for?" To what end would you be practicing this type of law with those people? Is it to make money? Is it to make enough money so that you can afford to "do good"? To make the world a better place? Better for whom? You are likely to be both happier and more productive if you can articulate a larger goal to work toward.

Pushing yourself and your partners to clarify a distant goal may help you formulate some general and deep underlying purpose for your actions. Or, upon reflection, it might cause you to abandon that mid-distant goal for some other, and to revise your "next steps" so that they are more aligned with your distant vision.

Ask "by what means?" To move back from a distant purpose toward a mid-distant goal and some immediate objectives, we ask ourselves, "How? By what means?" Those who might like to work toward the vision of a federal government of the world can ask themselves how they might try to get there. What are some possible mid-distant goals that would indicate that they would be partway there? To decide what to do tomorrow they will need to identify some potential points en route between the vision of a distant future and today's reality. Such a mid-distant goal might be an organization ("World Federalists") to promote the vision. Other such intermediate goals might be books or courses that would demonstrate the desirability of the distant goal and create support for it.

ONE PERSON'S PURPOSE

The lawyer who found himself without a motivating purpose did not have to accept that situation. He could have chosen to formulate a purpose for himself, instead of looking to others to provide one for him. It might look like this:

Long-term vision.

In five years I will have started in solo practice that focuses on the specialty I like best: intellectual property rights in software.

Mid-term goal.

In two years I will be working with three clients in this area and will have brought two clients of my own to the firm. Lawyers who know me will think of me as specializing in intellectual property. I will have published a short article on a software copyright case.

Objectives of my next steps.

By the end of this month I will have done such good work on my current case that the managing partner agrees to have me do the oral argument. I will get myself assigned to that new case Stan brought in by doing some extra research after hours and impressing him with some good suggestions. I will have joined the bar committee on copyright and trademark.

SECOND, CLARIFY A VISION OF JOINTLY USING THIS SKILL: EVERYONE HELPS FORMULATE A SET OF RESULTS TO ACHIEVE TOGETHER

Improving your personal skill at setting purposes is valuable, even if you do nothing more. It can also serve as a stepping-stone toward an audacious goal — getting a group to adopt better practices for the organization.

PROBLEM: WHEN WORKING WITH OTHERS, A MUDDY PURPOSE IS EVEN MORE OF A HINDRANCE

Just as you will get more done if you have a clear goal, you will be better off if your organization has a clear collective purpose. As the number of people who are working together rises, the importance of a clear, commonly understood purpose increases geometrically. If you are working alone without a purpose, you will likely get *something* done. When others join you, the lack of a clear, commonly understood purpose may prevent you from accomplishing anything. An organization without a clear idea of what it is trying to do is an organization in disarray.

The young partner at the law firm found his own efforts flagging because he lacked a clear understanding of his purpose. That was not the only consequence, or the worst. Over the next year he watched as the firm teetered on the brink of dissolution.

Three managing partners brought in most of the business and had the most influence in decisions. Andy pursued high-profile financiers as clients, and wanted to keep a stable of the brightest young attorneys partly idle so that he could swing into action on litigation making the front page of the *Wall Street Journal*. Stan pursued a national strategy of litigation against insurance companies that denied coverage for their industrial clients' environmental cleanup costs. He took on low-paying cases for municipalities with claims for environmental damage, trying to establish favorable precedents in strategically chosen state courts. Because these cases covered many years and large numbers of environmental damage sources, they required a huge investment of personnel to look through all the documentary evidence. Fred wanted all lawyers to work for full-fare clients to maximize profits per partner, a common measure of success in the industry. The three managing partners fought over these issues in firm meetings for years. Eventually one of them left the firm and took away a large part of the client base. By that time the young partner no longer cared. He had long since quit.

This sort of situation is distressingly common. Members of an organization feel no motivating purpose and are disaffected. Others try to pull the organization in different directions, without having an explicit discussion of what the firm should try to achieve. Stated purposes don't give the staff guidance on how to go about their jobs. What causes these problems?

Some causes are the same as those you observed in yourself. People react to the past, rarely looking forward. We have a vague purpose like "excellence" that does not provide us with guidance for our actions. Other causes are particular to working in a group.

Some Don't Understand Any Purpose

When someone new comes on board, we usually spend more time telling them what to do than why. That may save us some time in the short run, but when a new topic comes up the trainee will have to come back for more direction.

We Work at Cross Purposes

Often people work together with different understandings of what they want to achieve. Your next-door neighbor proposes that you jointly install a fence across the end of your yards to separate them from the adjacent field. You agree. You want to keep rabbits out of the garden, and are shocked when he has an eight-foot wood fence installed to block the noise and sight of a nearby highway. Rabbits squeeze under it easily.

It is possible to accomplish both purposes, if you start with a common understanding of them. The larger the number of people working together, the greater the risk that some will have conflicting objectives.

It Is Hard to Get Everyone Enlisted

Working in a group increases the peril of sloth. With others present, there are more distractions — you can socialize with colleagues or scheme against them. Moreover, the urgency to get things done is less powerful. Surely someone else will handle the problem. You can relax. The diminished sense of personal responsibility that we all feel in a crowd takes over. Social psychologists have found that the force generated by a team pulling a rope in a tug of war is usually far less than the sum of the individuals' strength.

VISION: A SET OF GOALS THAT GUIDES US AND MOTIVATES US, CREATED TOGETHER

A group will work better if they can use jointly the skill of setting purpose that you have developed for yourself. Like chefs in a large restaurant, different people in an organization will be pursuing different immediate objectives, all of which will later be combined in fulfillment of a larger purpose. The larger accomplishment is likely to be better to the extent that all understand the picture of which they are a part. And a task that seemed menial and dull can become well worth doing when you appreciate its contribution to a larger end — and you know that your colleagues appreciate it, too. President Kennedy once asked an old man sweeping the floor at Cape Canaveral, "What do you do here?" "We're sending a man to the moon," came the reply.

Joint brainstorming, discussion, drafting, and redrafting of different formulations serve to sharpen our purpose and make it a more useful guide. John Harvey-Jones, the former chairman of a giant international chemical company, ICI, described in his book *Making It Happen* how he and his board of directors used this method to set the direction for the company. They would have informal discussions doing "tremendous amounts of work on flip charts." The outcome of perhaps three days' work was "often no more than ten points on a flip chart, and we would consider that a good rate of striking." In his view they reached in that way "a shared view and a commitment to that view, which is usually of a different order to that which we can achieve by any other means." Joint work on defining purposes greatly reduces the risk that we will be working at cross purposes.

Everyone Helps Formulate the Goals to Work Toward

Members of an organization will understand its purpose best when they have helped create it. You may think, "This is crazy. A big company can't invite every employee to a meeting to set goals. And what would ensure that the goals chosen by the employees will be in tune with what the board and the shareholders want?" You have a point. It is difficult. But it is not impossible. A useful purpose is difficult to formulate. The larger the number of people who are working together, the harder it is to have everyone participate in formulating the purpose of their joint efforts. And some members of an organization, those at the top, have special responsibility for shaping its vision and goals.

One rule of thumb is that each member of an organization should help set the goals for which he or she will be responsible. When a long-term vision or mid-range goal is established by senior management, the workers at each level can plan the way in which they can best make that vision a reality.

One of the most valuable aspects of formulating goals at different points in time — which is to say, at different levels of contribution to a larger task — is that it allows more people to take part in a relatively efficient process of setting purposes. The board of directors may set the long-range vision. Perhaps middle management may set mid-term goals. Individual employees may set the next steps that they will accomplish en route to those larger purposes.

One task for the managers is to check that the immediate, personal goals set by each subgroup or employee are aligned with the long-term vision and sufficiently ambitious to challenge the employee. Someone needs to ask the questions, "For what purpose?" and "By what means?" on behalf of the organization. Monitoring the goals and purposes set by each employee also provides a method of ensuring that they understand the larger purposes toward which they are working.

Everyone Learns Colleagues' Immediate Objectives

Another advantage of setting purposes together is that each person will learn not only the steps that he will take next, but also the goals toward which his colleagues will be working. When you know a colleague's goal, you can provide information and resources that will help him achieve it. You can stay out of his way by avoiding actions that would interfere.

Having Helped Formulate Objectives, Most Are More Committed

Getting employees to take an organization's goals as their own is one problem that every organization faces. How can we get workers — whether on the shop floor or in the executive suite — to feel real commitment to the goals toward which they are working?

The easiest way to get a person to treat the organization's goals as her own is to have her help set the organization's goals. If you work out how you will support a larger goal, you are more likely to think it is important. If someone helps set a performance goal she will think it is reasonable — she can hardly argue that the firm is expecting too much of her if she is the one who laid out the guidelines.

"How can we make this happen?" To see how the process works, look at a small example. Imagine a small consulting organization that offers negotiation advice. The founder of the firm has an idea he likes, and requests that three of the young consultants be assigned to use about half their work time to help him. He calls a meeting.

FOUNDER: I've been thinking that we should do something about violence in schools. But we can't go to every school. A jazzy video that kids would watch could teach the same points. And a lot of schools that can't afford to hire us could afford a few hundred dollars for a video series. We might do well financially by doing good. And some entertainment companies that are being attacked for showing sex and violence on television might like to support such a project to improve their image. Well, what would we need to do on the way? How could we make that happen?

CONSULTANT 1: I'd suggest we start with the first video in a series. We could shop that around to customers, and if it sold we'd have some money to invest in the rest of it.

CONSULTANT 2: And what if they don't like it? We'll have invested a lot of time in a dead end.

CONSULTANT 1: It would involve the same principles we teach all the time. We could use it in other courses, too. We could figure out examples that would illustrate points in existing standard courses.

CONSULTANT 3: Before we do that we would need to get a partner to foot production expenses. Who do we know that could get us in the door at a production company?

CONSULTANT 2: I'll ask our board members. They're supposed to be well connected. And we will need something to show these people to pitch the idea.

CONSULTANT 1: We could shoot a version on low-cost video.

CONSULTANT 3: With our acting talents? Don't real movie people show producers a script?

FOUNDER: Good idea. Would you be willing to take a crack at drafting a script?

CONSULTANT 3: Um, all right . . .

After more work they adopt the following purpose:

A distant vision.

In five years we will have a division that produces instructional videos to teach high school students how to get more through negotiation than they can through violence. The series of videos will be in use in many schools throughout the country. Teens who have watched the videos will be statistically less likely to be arrested for violent crimes. Our division will supply the intellectual content, and it will have a strategic partnership with an organization that has expertise in producing and distributing entertainment (and perhaps educational) media. The project will generate enough revenue to support itself and help fund its expansion.

A mid-term goal.

Within two years we will have produced one ten- to fifteen-minute video on alternatives to violence that will teach a few simple lessons, which will be valuable even if the rest of the series is never created. It could be used as part of several existing courses. Further, it will provide a basis for designing other installments in a series.

Immediate objectives.

Within three months we will have:

- Scheduled meetings with influential executives in at least two media companies (such as Disney, Paramount, Time Warner, and Nickelodeon) to interest them in the idea (to be done by founder).

- A draft proposal that will include an outline of the series (Consultant 1).
- A draft script for an introductory episode (Consultants 2 and 3).

If the practice of jointly formulating purposes seems like an attractive and useful one to you, the next question is, What could you do to bring it closer?

THEN LEAD: IMPROVE PURPOSE-SETTING IN YOUR ORGANIZATION

Armed with a vision of better collaboration in setting purposes, you can direct your attention to making it happen. You can get better practices applied by your subordinates, your coworkers, and even your boss. Depending on the circumstances you can choose the tactic that seems likely to be most effective. It will not be easy. Attempts to ease a problem will sometimes make it worse.

Recall the young law partner whose firm lacked a clear understanding of its purpose. He did try to help. Unfortunately the tactics he chose were not effective.

His first approach was to register his dissatisfaction with the way the leading partners were struggling among themselves. During a partnership meeting called to deal with an unexpected dip in the firm's earnings, he bravely addressed the managing partners: "You guys complain that we aren't making enough money, and you want the young attorneys to put in more hours. But Andy keeps putting people on pro bono cases that don't earn us any money. And Stan stockpiles lawyers working on background research so that he'll have them available if he lands a new client. Don't blame us for the low profits. If you really want the firm to earn more, then you'll have to give up your own indulgences." The young partner was widely congratulated by the other lawyers at his level for speaking unmentionable truths. However, the senior partners did not change their behavior toward staffing cases, except to direct particularly unattractive assignments toward the young partner.

He thought to himself, "I just attacked them for their current behavior, without giving them any positive suggestions. No wonder they dug in their heels." His next approach was to tell them his solution. At the next partnership meeting he came prepared with his own statement of purpose for the firm. He passed it around and moved for a vote to adopt it. Without even looking at the proposed statement of purpose, the most senior partner said, "We make you partner, and the next thing you think you're in charge. Where were you when I founded this firm?" The young partner got his vote, and lost by a big margin.

What would you do? Stop reading for a moment. Think about the situation. What different approaches could you try? After you have planned an approach, look over our suggestions. We can't claim that ours are better than yours (especially since we don't know what yours are), but these should give you some more ideas to think about.

Know the Purpose for Every Task

So what could you do to make your organization work better? Start small. Even minor tasks ought to be done for a clearly understood purpose. So whenever you get an instruction from above or a request from a colleague — find out the purpose. *Ask for data.* You may be running for a newspaper because your boss told you to get one. To accomplish that task well, you need to know the purpose. And rather than just asking your boss: "Why?" (which might stimulate the response: "Because I told you to!"), get her to appreciate the *purpose* of your inquiry.

Perhaps you could say something like, "Yes, ma'am. And it might help me get the right kind of paper quickly if I know the purpose for which you want it." Both cause and purpose are important. Similarly when you initiate some activity yourself, *offer data*. When you issue an order or request, take a moment to explain the purpose for which you want something done.

When you have that part down, you are ready to move on to bigger things. There are more ambitious — and more difficult — approaches designed to influence the entire organization's understanding of its purpose.

Work to Improve the Organization's Substantive Purpose

There are usually two problems: the substance of the purpose itself may be lacking, and it may have been created using a process that discourages the rank and file from taking ownership of it. We will address how you could tackle each problem in turn.

Ask for data: find the thinking behind the current statement of purpose. If your firm has a bland statement of purpose that doesn't motivate the employees, or a vague one that cannot be translated into concrete action, the first step is to find out more. Don't assume that you know all you need to know. The problem may be that no one has thought through what makes a statement of purpose useful, or it may merely be a question of articulating the ideas that the organization's leaders have. There may be a more detailed version of the purpose that hasn't been communicated to you yet. There may be obstacles to forming a more useful purpose of which you are not aware. First you need to develop more information about the problem. That information is not only for your use. As you go to others for help finding out more, you will give them the opportunity to start working on the problem as well.

In the case of the young associate, he might go to each of the three senior partners and ask some questions:

- "Where does our mission statement come from? Who wrote it?"
- "What does it mean?"
- "What did you think about including that was dropped?"
- "What is it about that vision that you find attractive?"
- "When was it created? Have you learned anything to change your thinking?"

There are two possible outcomes to this line of questioning. You may get satisfying, inspiring information about the purpose that helps you guide your efforts. In that case, you merely need to communicate that information to others like you in the firm. Or your questions might expose a lack of serious, motivating purpose. That doesn't mean you have to stop asking questions. It does mean that your questions should guide your boss toward helpful topics to think about, and that you will have to give him space to think before answering.

This is one case where having a lower rank on the totem pole makes it easier to influence others. No one can blame you for wanting to know more about the organization's purpose. And your questions can prompt the leadership to think about exactly the same issues that you would recommend as an agenda for a purpose-setting meeting. You can frame your questions as the sort of thing that an inexperienced person would like explained to him, rather than as a challenge to the competence of the people who designed the purpose. The first thing you will need is a good-sized chunk of time from someone senior enough to make a difference. Return to the example of the law firm. The associate might try something like this:

"Hello, sir. I'm wondering if I could make an appointment to talk with you about our company goals. I have some questions about them and how I can make sure that my work here helps bring them closer. I guess it would take something like half an hour or an hour.

"I guess I'm a little behind the curve on understanding our purpose, and I have a hard time figuring out some of the lingo that business people use. If 'being known for the highest standards of excellence in the practice of law' is our vision, where does that mean we ought to be in five years? For example, would we rather increase the number of lawyers by thirty because we are getting more clients, or would we be winning a higher proportion of our cases? Or settling a higher proportion of cases?"

Once you have helped your boss to articulate a tangible goal, you can press for nearer and farther goals in line with it. "Okay, if that's our goal for five years, what should have happened by the end of this year?" "But why would we want that? Where would that get us?" "I'm trying to figure out a nearer goal that I could press toward in the meantime. How about something like . . . "

Hopefully, the result will be a first draft of a set of purposes across several points in time. It won't be perfect. In fact, you don't want it to be. Right now that purpose is only shared by you and your boss. There needs to be room for it to change if you are going to leverage the result of that meeting into something bigger. You could start by asking: "Would it be all right if I type up these targets and show them around? It might help some of the other younger people like me who need to see the vision translated into simple, down-to-earth results. And maybe some of the other senior folks could add something to it." Your memo might start a conversation throughout the firm, without your ever having done anything more offensive than ask questions and write down the results.

In addition to prodding others to think about these questions, you want to send a message to your superiors: "I understand that you know more the firm than I, and I want to learn from you." If you succeed in transmitting that message, few superiors will object.

Offer data and diagnosis: report your own reaction. Your first attempt may not go so smoothly. Perhaps the higher-ups will not make time to meet with you, not seeing any urgency in your questions. Perhaps they don't understand that there is any problem: "We already did what that consultant told us and wrote a statement of purpose. It's right there on the wall. What's wrong with that?"

Don't be easily discouraged. If you find that the firm's stated purpose is not particularly inspiring or helpful in making decisions, it is likely that others may share the same feeling. That is important data for the firm's management. In most organizations, higher-ups never learn that there is anything lacking in purposes they state. Telling them that the stated purpose isn't good enough may make them feel attacked. Since they are powerful people, most employees prefer not to risk antagonizing them. Further, dedication to the organization's purpose is taken as a sign of a loyal, industrious worker. Admitting that one does not feel committed to a particular statement of purpose requires courage.

You could go to one of the senior partners and say something like:

"I'm a little worried about how this might sound, since I don't want to seem like a malcontent. I'll say it anyway. I don't know what to make of the statement of purpose that's hanging in the lobby. I look at it when I'm thinking about how I can make a contribution. I guess I'm not clear on what 'excellence in the practice of law' is. I'm not sure what practical steps I can take to get us there. To me, at least, the statement seems rather abstract. Since I don't know what it means it doesn't help me when I'm pulling an all-nighter and wondering, 'Why am I doing this?'

"I think there might be others who think the same way. You might get more work out of us, even better work, if we had an explanation of what we are working toward."

You will want to frame your remarks in terms of the effect the stated purpose has on you, rather than as a judgment whether it a good purpose or not. The approach is to *offer data* that the purpose does not have a motivating effect on you, and share a *diagnosis* as to why that is. Sharing the diagnosis explains why you feel unmoved by the mission statement without that fact reflecting badly on you. It directs attention toward ways of improving the statement of purpose, instead of toward your "bad attitude." To a senior partner puzzling over how to motivate young lawyers to work harder, a diagnosis to work with might be a welcome relief.

Offer direction: suggest turning a vague vision into tangible goals. If you find that asking questions doesn't work, or if you feel comfortable that your bosses and colleagues will not resent your giving them direct advice, you can try offering explicit directions — not about what the purpose should be, but about a helpful format that a purpose can follow. In the case of our law firm, the toughest problem the firm faced was not lack of purpose, but deeply conflicting ideas about what the purpose should be. You don't want to get caught up in a battle over the substance of the purpose.

You might go to see one of the three top partners:

YOU: I think that the problems about allocating attorney time aren't just tactical disagreements. It seems like there are different views about the basic direction of the firm. Does that sound right?

PARTNER: Yeah. But the immediate issue is to get those guys to give us more people.

YOU: Maybe we need to start with a plan for where we want the firm to be in five years instead of whether you or Andy gets the next associate who's available. Then we could work backward to a plan for this month.

PARTNER: Just what kind of plan do you have in mind?

YOU: Well, I'm not sure. I think that you and Stan and Andy know more about that than I do. If you want I could write up a draft as a starting point, but I don't have any fixed ideas about what it should be.

PARTNER: That's not going to solve the problem of getting the billable hours up.

YOU: Not right now, anyway. Over time it might make people work harder if they had some target in mind that they were working toward.

PARTNER: Maybe.

YOU: What could we do to make that happen? If we tell Stan and Andy that we want to think about our long-term purpose they might think it was a maneuver to get them to agree to your plan.

PARTNER: Hmm. We could start by . . .

In practice I am preceding my suggested *direction* with the *data* (observed difficulties in allocating staff time) and *diagnosis* (different views on which our goals should be) on which I base it.

Offer a do next: propose the specifics of a meeting. Creation of a better set of purposes will not happen by itself. Someone needs to organize a specific proposal to make it happen. You could think through a specific action plan that would get it started. To reduce the risk that one or more of the three managing partners will react negatively to your audacity in offering a plan, you could prepare a draft memo to them and arrange to discuss it with another widely respected partner to obtain her advice. You might prepare one draft to be sent directly over your name and a variation, if she thinks it wiser, that might be sent over her name. That draft might be along the following lines:

"One of our younger partners has convinced me that some of our current problems stem from a lack of clarity about our long-term goals for the firm. The three of you have been so busy with current cases that I am sure you have had little time to meet and clarify long-range goals.

"I would like to volunteer to take on some of that burden. Could we have a preliminary meeting of the four of us? I might facilitate a discussion of where each of you would like to see the firm, say, five years hence. What might be a snapshot of the firm at that time? Then, what might it look like halfway there? And where would you like to see the firm at the end of this year — a short-term goal that would be moving us all in the direction you would like to see us take? After hearing your views I will try to prepare a rough draft for you three to consider.

"I have checked with your secretaries, and all three of you appear to be available next Thursday afternoon. I am holding the conference room on the 39th floor in the event that you think such a discussion might be worthwhile.

"It is not my expectation that one discussion will produce a clear and agreed picture of where the firm should be going, but a private talk among you about the results you would like to see in the future might help you clarify our goals in a way that will make it easier to resolve current issues.

"If you would rather meet alone, please let me know. I am simply offering a suggestion and my services."

It will surely not be easy for the three senior partners to agree on future goals. But the chances are much better if they explicitly address the problem, instead of hiding from it. In fact, the result may be that the firm decides that some people will split off to pursue goals that motivate them but not others. Better for that decision to come as a conscious choice than to have some storm away in frustration after spending years in an organization that does not serve their purposes.

Do something: draft an illustrative set of goals. It may also be useful to take a first cut at a better set of goals. If nothing else, your draft could serve as an example of the type of goals that would be useful for the organization. Don't ask for approval of your draft — rather, send it around to a few colleagues and ask them to mark it up. They can improve it, or come up with something else entirely.

In fact, even if you are sure exactly what the organization's goals should be, you should probably submit a draft that is rough or incomplete. Let others have the satisfaction of sharpening and improving a statement of the group's goals. If you can help get better goals established without being resented, you will have good cause to be satisfied.

Improve the Process by Getting Everyone Involved in Setting Subsidiary Goals

Ask for data: is everyone sufficiently committed to the goal? You will not get far persuading the powers that be to adopt a process for getting workers more committed if they think everyone is already committed enough. You could direct your boss's attention toward that problem, and possibly learn that it isn't the problem you think it is.

> **YOU:** Chief, do you think that everyone around here is working hard enough? Are they as committed to the company purposes as you would like?

Offer a diagnosis: someone else's goals don't motivate me as much as my own. One problem with merely looking for data is that it is tempting to find unproductive diagnoses for commitment problems. Most times when we think of people who are uncommitted we jump to the conclusion that they are lazy or malingering, rather than that there might be a problem with the commitment they are being asked to make.

> **BOSS:** Well, they're not bad, but I suppose it could be better. What's on your mind?
>
> **YOU:** I'm thinking that one factor is whether people see the goals we're working toward as just the management's goals or as their own.
>
> **BOSS:** Sure that's a factor, but what can we do? It's nice if the company goals line up with the ones people have on

their own, but we can't change the company goals to match what people want.

you: I know what you mean. We don't want to choose goals because they will be easier for the employees. At the same time, if they had some input in refining and editing the goals, they would have more ownership of them. The same goal moves me more if I helped make it than if I didn't.

boss: But how can it be the same goal if you helped make it?

Offer direction: let everyone help set goals. Your boss may work out a good plan for getting everyone involved in setting purposes on his own. If not, you can be ready with a few ideas for him to build on.

you: We could have a set of goals at different times. You could map out the big ones for us, and then have everyone come up with what they are going to do to see that we get there.

boss: What if they just set themselves easy goals?

you: You could have them nominate goals for your approval without giving up your authority. After all, you're still the boss. You would just let them work out the steps on the way to where you want us to go. What would be wrong with a plan like that?

Helping an organization to adopt a clear purpose composed of tangible results at several points in time will not usher in a utopia. It will help. It will solve some problems, and serve as a platform to tackle others. A good statement of purpose is like a cornerstone that supports a whole edifice of collaboration.

If you can help make your organization's purpose stronger, you have done well, and deserve to be congratulated. If your team already has a clearly stated and useful purpose, don't worry. There are plenty of other elements involved in getting things done, elements that deserve attention.

4 THINKING

HARNESS THE POWER OF ORGANIZED THOUGHT

Sometimes you are clear on your purpose but you just don't know how to achieve it. Or you choose an approach that turns out to be ineffective. If something like that is the case, you will want to work on the second element, THINKING.

Even when working alone, most people's thinking jumps from one idea to another, rather than progressing forward in an orderly way. When working with others the confusion is compounded. Disorganized thinking is most damaging when it disrupts an important business task. Yet the chaos of joint thinking is perhaps most apparent when we work on something ordinary, because we are less distracted by the seriousness of the problem. Take, for example, an office Christmas party. Discussion is likely to proceed in "grasshopper fashion," jumping from topic to topic:

"How about inviting spouses this year?"
"What about those who aren't married?"
"I thought that last year Mr. Jenkins, for one, got drunk."
"I, for one, left hungry."

"People are supposed to know everyone in the office, but the older ones don't."

"It shouldn't be called a Christmas party because of our Jewish colleagues."

"I never know who to call by their first name."

"Isn't it 'whom'?"

"Isn't who whom?"

"Skip it."

"When is the party going to be held?"

Each person at the table knows that this pattern is not productive. Yet each continues to play a part that allows it to go on. The result in most organizations is wasted time and poor decisions.

There is no answer book for the situations that you and I encounter in a day's work. Each of us has to face new problems, and create new solutions, every day. And when you are working with colleagues, they have information and ideas that could help. You will get little benefit from them by ignoring their thinking, cutting them off, or spending time on irrelevant topics. Two heads are better than one, but only if they have some way to coordinate themselves. To organize your own thinking is hard enough. To organize joint thinking is more difficult.

Before you can work out how to improve joint thinking you need to sharpen your own. The first part of this chapter proposes that you develop a personal skill. That skill is thinking systematically, starting with the facts and ending up with what to do. The second part of the chapter proposes a vision — what it would look like to have a number of people use this skill together. The final part of the chapter suggests a number of ways in which one individual — you — might laterally lead colleagues toward that vision.

FIRST, DEVELOP A PERSONAL SKILL: THINK SYSTEMATICALLY

PROBLEM: WHEN THINKING IS HAPHAZARD, A COMPLEX TASK CAN BE OVERWHELMING

If you find it difficult to get things done, it is often because your thinking is disorganized. It is hard to know where to start. You think in circles, coming back to thoughts you have had before. You skip important steps. After thinking of one idea it is hard to keep looking. Not only are you likely to jump around among different subjects of logical analysis — such as plans, facts, strategies, and causes of difficulty — you are often unclear what you want your thinking to produce. An idea? An evaluation? A decision? And it isn't only you. It happens to all of us. Why is our thinking so often rudderless?

In school we were taught a great many answers, but not how to think. Most of us learn no framework to organize thinking so that questions come in a useful order. That leaves us trying to generate good answers without knowing good questions. Trying to be a clear thinker without a set of standard questions is like trying to be a carpenter without a hammer or a saw.

PRESCRIPTION: USE A BOX OF "TOOLS" TO AID CLEAR THINKING

To organize your thinking in a way that helps you get things done, you first want a framework of big questions that offers a logical sequence. And within that framework, you will want other tools to help produce better thinking.

A FRAMEWORK FOR THINKING SYSTEMATICALLY: THE CIRCLE CHART

Working in an organization, you are overloaded with practical problems. Naturally you look for quick and practical solutions. You tend to jump from the symptom of a problem, be it a drop in revenue or a memo from your boss, to a specific next step. Others, with a more academic frame of mind, think in abstract terms. They analyze the world with descriptive theory. They generate prescriptive theory, suggesting general guidelines for the future. We can divide concrete, specific thinking from abstract, general thinking. Another big division is between thinking about the past and thinking about the future. Some want to understand and explain what already is. Others are more interested in what sort of future we want, and what we should do next.

We can represent these distinctions by taking a piece of paper and dividing it horizontally. Conceptual thinking about causes and general approaches goes in the upper half of the chart; thinking about specific practical events on the ground goes in the lower half of the chart. Now divide it vertically. Thinking about the past up to the present is on the left side of the chart. Thinking about the future is on the right side. The resulting four-quadrant Circle Chart divides thinking into four basic categories:

- DATA — the factual situation, or problem.
- DIAGNOSIS — an analysis of causes of the situation.
- DIRECTION — one or more general approaches for overcoming those causes.
- DO NEXT — specific steps or plans for implementing an approach.

If you want to accomplish as much as you can, all four kinds of thinking are important. Do not limit your thinking either to the past or to the future. Bring theory to bear on practice, and use practice to improve theory.

These categories are simple, useful, and easy to learn. When you use the Circle Chart, you are never stuck on how to get

THE CIRCLE CHART

A Framework for Systematic Thinking
and some subsidiary TOOLS for clear thinking
(Start in the lower left-hand quadrant)

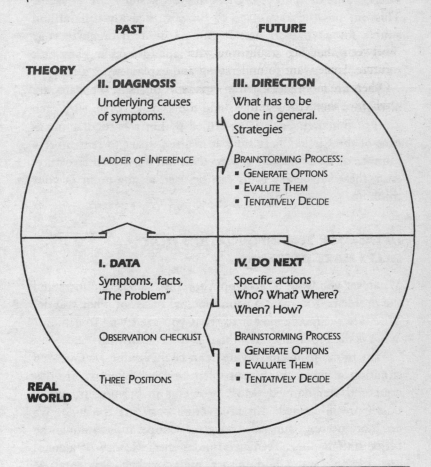

PAST   FUTURE

THEORY

II. DIAGNOSIS   **III. DIRECTION**

Underlying causes   What has to be
of symptoms.   done in general.
                              Strategies

LADDER OF INFERENCE   BRAINSTORMING PROCESS:
                              ▪ GENERATE OPTIONS
                              ▪ EVALUATE THEM
                              ▪ TENTATIVELY DECIDE

I. DATA   **IV. DO NEXT**

Symptoms, facts,   Specific actions
"The Problem"   Who? What? Where?
                              When? How?

OBSERVATION CHECKLIST   BRAINSTORMING PROCESS
                              ▪ GENERATE OPTIONS
                              ▪ EVALUATE THEM
THREE POSITIONS   ▪ TENTATIVELY DECIDE

REAL
WORLD

started thinking about a problem — whether it is a challenge in your substantive work or the problem of getting others to work together more effectively with you and with one another.

The Circle Chart is a good overall structure for relating different kinds of thinking. Other logical systems are possible. This one has the advantage of being sufficiently general and simple for anyone to use. It can be used to organize your thinking to develop soundly based plans for tackling any task or difficulty.

Each kind of thinking has its own challenges. This chapter also offers some helpful ideas and tools to assist you with each kind of thinking. Each is described within a particular quadrant of the Circle Chart since it is often easier to remember a number of items if each is placed within an overall structure. And, these subsidiary tools can be used at any point in your thinking.

DATA: LOOK FOR INFORMATION THAT HELPS MAKE DECISIONS

Whatever you want to accomplish, a first step is to understand the problem. You want a sound factual basis for what you do. What are the facts relevant to what you are trying to achieve? What is the problem at hand that is to be dealt with?

The term "problem solving" can be misleading. It implies a situation in which both a problem and a "solution" are discrete and well-defined. Most problems in business or public policy are ill-defined: our production costs are too high. We are not meeting our sales targets. Cooperation among the office staff is poor. Teenagers under the influence of alcohol are driving cars. Children are malnourished. Students are poorly educated.

Your goal is rarely to find the one elegant solution, such as to a jigsaw or crossword puzzle. It is to get things done — to make improvement in the right direction — such as lower unit costs, higher sales, more effective cooperation, fewer drunk drivers, better nourishment, or better education.

"Problem" also suggests a broken machine — everything was fine until the problem occurred. It is better to think of it as a challenge, or an opportunity. For example, you have a highly productive factory, but would like to do even better. "Problem" simply means there is a gap between the current situation and a better situation that you can imagine.

As you collect and examine data your role is similar to that of a medical doctor examining a patient who doesn't feel well. The doctor wants to learn more. What are the symptoms? Where is the pain? Has the patient felt like this before? Has he done anything unusual recently? As the doctor collects data, she will check the reliability of the patient's observations (and her own), and organize the relevant information.

There Is Too Much Information to Handle

We are constantly swamped with information. "Information overload" existed long before electronic communication. There is no getting around the fact that we can look at only a small fraction of what there is to see. An American arranged to meet his wife at the Melbourne Cricket Ground to watch a game of Australian Rules Football. When she did not arrive he began walking around the stadium, where some 30,000 football fans were waiting. After walking through the crowd for a while he realized that he must have *seen* her from a distance, but he couldn't *notice* her among the vast number of faces. The problem is not observing more, but rather how to sort the nuggets of helpful information out of the mountain of dross. There will always be a lot more to know about your colleagues and what you are doing than you will be able to take in. The crucial task is selecting what to look for.

Everyone has "filters" to select the information that

receives their attention. If we do not consciously choose them we fall back on unconscious ones. Typically these default rules for selecting data limit the useful information we receive. Like a magician's sleight of hand, they direct attention away from the true action.

Are you biased toward vivid data? We all pay undue attention to a good story. Information that has an emotional impact gobbles up attention. Dry information is ignored. As you try to accomplish something you may find that the bankruptcy of one competitor holds your attention more than an improved product being marketed by another. At work no one has packaged important information to make it easy to take in.

Do you give undue weight to quantifiable data? The very phrase "It doesn't count" implies that unless one can put a number to something it is unimportant. It is easier to look at information that can be reduced to a single figure. "Sales are up 2 percent this quarter." Reality is not always so simple. "Several customers — I don't know how many — have complained about our responding slowly to telephone calls."

Do you think that what you know is more important than what you don't? We often equate the information we have with the information that should guide a decision. This creates two difficulties. First, we assume that what we don't already know isn't worth knowing. We stop looking for information when there may still be important things to learn. Secondly, we think that because we have a certain piece of information, it should figure into the decision: "If it is true, it is relevant." Years are spent fighting over what happened yesterday for every day that is spent figuring out what ought to be done tomorrow.

Are you trapped in your own point of view? Russians have a saying that "everyone looks at the world from the bell tower of his own village." We all know that we tend to judge ourselves more charitably than we judge others. You notice your own contributions to a success more than those of others. You tend to minimize, even to yourself, the role you played in a failure. Because we focus on data that favor us or cast others in a bad light, we neglect large amounts of relevant information.

Aim Your Observation

Telling yourself to be more observant is not particularly helpful. You could spend all your time observing without any guarantee that the data you gathered would be relevant.

It is possible to direct your view toward useful data. You can consciously affect the way your brain gathers data. Return to the example of the American at the Australian football game. Frustrated, almost despairing of finding his wife in the crowd, he remembered that she wore a distinctive green jacket. He scanned the crowd for people wearing that particular color. Out of thousands of fans there were now only a few dozen candidates for closer examination. By sensitizing himself to particular data he quickly found his wife. One approach to gathering data is to pick a sensitizing lens that will make important information stand out. Just as you can sensitize your mind to notice a particular color in a crowd, you can sensitize it to certain subjects.

Using a lens is tricky. If the wife had not worn the green jacket that day, using that lens would have made the situation worse, not better. We want a lens that will guide us to look for important data whether or not it is vivid or quantifiable, that will push us beyond the constraints of our training and prior experience. Yet it should not prevent us from gathering relevant information, whether or not it is highlighted by the lens we are using.

What Data Do You Want? Use an OBSERVATION CHECKLIST

The particular data to which you want to sensitize yourself will depend on the task. You may want to prepare an observation checklist, reminding yourself of the kind of data that will be relevant, the kind that may be out there, and the kind of lens or filter that you might use to sort out what you want to collect from all that you are likely to encounter.

We cannot offer you a checklist for your substantive work, but we think the following one will help you look at the way you and your colleagues are collaborating:

Purpose
   Have we formulated a list of goals to be accomplished at different points in time?

Thinking
   Are we moving logically from symptoms through diagnosis to planning?
   Do we have tools to help us observe how we collaborate?
   Are we testing our theories against the data?
   Are we trying to create the same products of thinking?

Learning
   Are we regularly reviewing and learning from experience?
   Are we moving quickly between preparation, action, and review?

Engagement
   Does every task have someone responsible for it?
   Does each team member have a challenging responsibility?
   Are we inviting and welcoming the ideas of all?

Feedback
   Do we regularly offer appreciation and support?
   Do we exchange specific coaching?

No matter how stimulating and helpful a checklist may be, all data that you collect is likely to suffer from the fact that you are a single observer with limited vision and with the biases of any human being.

How to Escape Your Own Bias? Try the THREE POSITIONS

You can work around, or even make use of, biases that distort your observations. To offset the self-serving bias that everyone experiences, look at significant issues from three different angles or points of view: yours, the other side's, and that of some neutral third party.

The first position: "me." Ask yourself: What is my general perception of the situation? How do things look from here? From my particular and personal point of view, what is the available data? What seems to me to be important?

In addition to looking out, you want to look at yourself. Are you emotionally involved, frustrated, angry? Do you tend to be overconfident, selfish, or feel guilty about taking care of yourself? What are some of your deeply held opinions? What are some of your biases? What professional point of view, experiences, or special interests may cause you to ignore some things and give undue importance to others? Are you likely to be looking at this situation through a filter or, to continue the metaphor, through rose-colored glasses, binoculars, or a microscope? You want to be aware of the extent to which looking from your position shapes the data.

Don't abandon your point of view, or assume that it is wrong. Some people fall into the trap of giving up their own opinions once they see that other views could have some validity. There is no need to surrender your own perceptions. You do want to recognize that you have a partial view. The more aware you are of your limitations, the better an observer you become.

The second position: "them." They second task is to consider the perspective of your coworkers. You want to put yourself in their shoes and try to see the situation as it looks to them. If there are many with whom you will be working, identify one or two key people and try to look at the joint project as it may appear to each of them.

Imagine that you are this other person and ask all the questions you asked yourself when observing from the first position. If you are considering your boss, what is she worried about? What are some of her standard approaches? Her biases?

Looking from a second position involves taking advantage of inherent biases in a constructive way. You will still have a self-serving bias, but it will serve your imagined role. You will probably focus on data that makes your boss look good. You will still have a confirmation bias, but it will be finding data that confirms *her* views. From this point of view you will have a better chance of observing the data that stands out to her, data that you would otherwise overlook. Not only will you become aware of different aspects of the situation you are both in, you will learn something else: a better approximation of where her mind is.

Certainly it is a lot easier to say "look at things from their point of view" than to do so. But there are several techniques that are surprisingly useful in getting a better understanding of how another sees things:

Role reversal.

One way to go is the way an actor does. Imagine yourself to be the other person. Try to think and speak as he does. You can have a friend or colleague interview you while you play the absent party. You may even want to reenact a conversation with you playing the absent party and with your friend portraying you, the way you typically behave.

Currently perceived choice.

Another tool uses pencil and paper to illuminate how things look from the second position. Put yourself in the other party's shoes and consider the decision he would have make to agree with you. For example, "Should I agree with Bob's proposal to give more authority to local managers?" Then list in parallel columns the probable consequences, as that party is likely to perceive them, of saying "yes" and those of saying "no." You will likely discover that he has good reasons to say "no." Once you see more clearly what concerns he may have about the proposal, it will be easier to formulate a revised proposal that meets those concerns.

These methods do require an investment of time and thought, and it is not always worth the effort. You cannot make a detailed analysis of every person you deal with. Yet there are many situations in which it is well worth it. You may want to look at your boss's perspective — or a subordinate's — about your relationship. It is likely to be particularly useful in considering how to improve the collaboration when you need to get something done with someone from another department or organization. Taking the time to understand his point of view may well save time.

The third position: "high in the stands." You will also want to collect data that will offer perspective on the partisan views of the participants. In addition to the way a situation appears to those who are actively involved, you will want to understand how it might look to a spectator. To do so, visualize yourself watching a stage performance from the balcony, or taking the vantage of a "fly on the wall." Attempt to be objective. No doubt you will fall short, but you will get closer to an unbiased view. Both we in this book and Bill Ury in *Getting Past No* use "going to the balcony" as a powerful metaphor for stepping back and gaining perspective, a concept that was generated by Ronald Heifeitz — Harvard colleague, creative thinker, and excellent teacher.

A great soccer player does more than just "play the ball." He considers the whole field as it looks from high up in the stands. He has an eye out for what other players on both teams are doing and planning. He takes in the big picture. When you are "high in the stands" you have a chance to consider information that you may miss if you do nothing but keep your eye on the ball.

These techniques will not guarantee that you will observe all relevant data. They will help you do a better job. Gathering data, however, is not enough. You need to make sense of it, to explain the situation so that you can figure out what to do.

DIAGNOSIS: RATHER THAN REACT TO SYMPTOMS, STEP BACK AND LOOK FOR CAUSES

Diagnosis Is a Crucial Step in Problem Solving

Despite the importance of making a sound diagnosis, the busier we are, the more likely we are to omit it. When faced with a practical difficulty we tend to respond immediately with a practical solution. A school principal who realizes that most of her staff arrives late to weekly teaching meetings might respond by scheduling the meeting ten minutes later. If a factory is turning out flawed cars, a manager might assign more workers to inspect the product. These responses may or may not be effective. We can't tell unless we know what lies behind the disliked situation. What is causing staff to arrive late? What is causing the defects in the cars? If we don't take the time to ask what factors are causing the disliked symptoms, we may miss the best strategy for overcoming them.

The difference that a successful diagnosis makes cannot be overstated. In 1994 millions of refugees from Rwanda fled to Zaire and began dying in large numbers. Well-meaning relief officials made heroic efforts to deliver food to the suffering people. A few days later, these officials learned that the reason Rwandan refugees were dying was not starvation but cholera. They quickly switched their efforts from bringing in food to creating latrines and a sanitary water supply, saving thousands of lives.

An accurate diagnosis will often lead to a counterintuitive prescription. Consider this example: Stacy is an engineer at an international architectural firm with offices in many countries. She spends a lot of her time flying to meetings in Europe. The meetings go slowly and take far too much time. Frustrated, Stacy tries to speed things up by saying as little as possible and making her points quickly and succinctly. The European members of the firm seem dissatisfied. They frown when she speaks, and seem to question every point she makes. An American colleague tells her, "That's just the way Europeans are. They take their time." One diagnosis is that her frustration is caused by cultural differences. Another is that the French and German partners go slowly because they want to be perfectly sure that they understand what is said in the English-language meetings. In that case, Stacy might speed up the meetings by speaking more slowly.

Look for causes that you will be able to affect. As you diagnose a situation, remember to distinguish two quite different kinds of "causes": those that you can't change and those that you can. A doctor tells a patient that his life expectancy is less than his wife's, and that there are two basic causes: one, that he was born a man and not a woman; two, that he smokes and she does not. There is nothing that he can do about the first. He can do something about the second — stop smoking. The best advice is, Don't bemoan what you can't change, focus on what you can. Look for diagnoses about which you may be able to do something.

How to Test a Diagnosis? Use the LADDER OF INFERENCE

A diagnosis should be based on hard data. Too often we jump to a conclusion. You infer something that goes beyond the data you have. Others with whom you work jump to different conclusions. You need to test rigorously the relationship between the available data and the interpretations you build on it.

One of the most dangerous habits of mind is to exclude information that conflicts with our opinions. Reading a newspaper, each of us finds pleasure in a story that confirms our thinking. We tend to skip those that would suggest we have been in error. Consider journals of political opinion. We all suspect that the average reader of *The National Review* is more likely to be a right-wing conservative who enjoys reading opinions he shares than a left-wing liberal seeking to understand and learn from a different point of view. By and large, people choose magazines that confirm their opinions. The same selective filtering takes place as we walk around an office or a factory floor. We see what we want to see.

Once we have jumped to a poorly founded conclusion, it is difficult to step back to firmer ground. Few of us enjoy realizing that we made a mistake. The easiest way to avoid that unpleasant sensation is to ignore or dismiss information that doesn't fit into our current thinking.

A good practice for dealing with differences between conclusions you have drawn and those of others is to articulate the relationship between facts you observe and conclusions you draw. It helps to make your chain of reasoning visible, to yourself and to colleagues. You can use a simple tool called the LADDER OF INFERENCE, developed by the organizational behavior theorists Chris Argyris, Robert Putnam, and Diana Smith. That ladder can be simplified to involve three rungs:

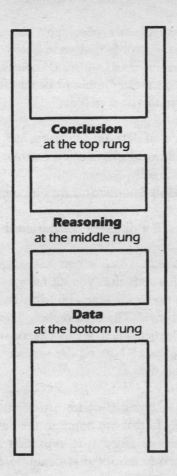

Conclusion
at the top rung

Reasoning
at the middle rung

Data
at the bottom rung

- CONCLUSIONS at the top.
- REASONING as the middle rung.
- DATA at the bottom.

   To test your reasoning or to share it with others, go down the ladder and start with the data. In effect you are going back from your diagnosis in Quadrant II to Quadrant I to check what you actually observed.

Data. Data are directly observable information — what was said or done — words that were heard, things that were seen, facial expressions, and so on. Of course, at any one time we are drawing on a finite amount of data from a far larger pool. Questions to ask here include:

- Which pieces of data am I focusing on?
- Is there additional information I would like to have that is possible to get?
- What available information am I leaving out?

You might reach a different conclusion if you started with different data.

Consider a case in which a boss has suggested to you and eight others on his staff that you all have a "mini-retreat" in the office over a two-hour lunch on Saturday. One staff member gasps, "Saturday?" The boss replies, "Yes. It will be good for us to get together when we can relax without the usual weekday interruptions." No one else says anything. That is the directly observable data.

Reasoning. Reasoning is concerned with the logic, deductions, and inferences that we apply to the data. We shape the data into a pattern or story. It is important to recognize that there are often many stories that could be formed from the same pieces of data, just as the same words could be rearranged to make other sentences.

People who start with the same data can reach different conclusions. In our example, the boss's reasoning may be that anyone on his staff who disagrees with his ideas will say so. Members of his staff may reason that openly disagreeing with a superior is a bad idea. They will express hearty approval of a plan they like, and go along in grudging silence with one they dislike.

Conclusions. Conclusions are the inferences that we draw by applying our reasoning to the observed data. In our example, the boss concludes that all nine of his staff, with the possible exception of one person, agree with his proposal. And now that he has answered her question, she also may agree.

Another in the group might conclude that since no one expressed approval of the proposal no one agrees with it; and since the boss heard the deafening silence that greeted his idea, he must realize that everyone else is opposed to it.

In such a situation, either conclusion may be wrong. Both may be wrong. A good way to resolve disagreement about such "facts" — in this case about whether people agree or disagree with the boss's proposal — is to go down the LADDER OF INFERENCE to the basically observed data and then check out the reasoning that led to such different conclusions. You need to go back to what actually happened, what was said or done and how it was said or done.

The value of exposing your reasoning and data to examination is illustrated by the account of a Connecticut banker who awakened a surgeon with a 2 A.M. phone call. He told the doctor, with whom he had dealt before, that his wife was having an acute appendicitis. The banker had some experience with appendicitis, and asked the doctor to meet them at the hospital immediately. The doctor listened to the banker's description of his wife's symptoms, then told him to give his wife a couple of aspirin and put her back to bed. He was confident that it was not an appendicitis. When asked for his reasoning, the doctor explained: "I removed your wife's appendix seven years ago, and no woman ever has a second appendix." The banker then explained the reasoning behind his concern: "Yes, Doctor, but some men have a second wife. Please meet us at the hospital."

The LADDER OF INFERENCE can be used to improve the accuracy of your diagnosis of a problem at work. When you have a tentative conclusion, look back for any data that would be inconsistent with it. Look for different conclusions that would explain the same data. Once you find a conclusion that stands up to examination you are ready to move on.

DIRECTION: INVENT CREATIVE APPROACHES

Understanding isn't enough. Thinking in Quadrants I and II should give you a good understanding of the what and why of the current situation. Moving to Quadrant III, shift your attention forward and develop one or more strategies for the future. Here you want to think about a general approach that will address your diagnosis. Your prescriptive hypothesis will depend on the descriptive one. If your current hypothesis is that a patient is suffering from headaches that are the result of poor vision, the strategy will be to prescribe glasses. If your diagnosis is that poor education is caused by lack of family support for doing homework, you will think about what you might do to increase parental support for their children's education.

Thinking in Quadrant III does not consist of detailed plans. It is at the level of inventing possible strategies, evaluating them, and tentatively deciding among them. At this stage you contrast needs with available resources and prepare broad plans accordingly.

Divide Thinking Among GENERATE — EVALUATE — DECIDE

We can distinguish three different *results* of thinking, whether that thinking is about diagnoses, broad strategies, or specific plans.

Possibilities.

Creative ideas are produced by brainstorming — by letting your mind range freely. Here the goal is to generate a number of ideas, looking for variety rather than quality.

Evaluations.

A quite separate mental process is that of weighing the merits of different ideas. Here the result will be arguments for and against a particular idea or an assessment of its worth.

Decisions.

A third form of thinking is deciding. When making decisions you formulate a possible decision and make a commitment — perhaps a tentative one. The product is a decision.

Consider Many Options Before Choosing

The most often neglected step is brainstorming — the imaginative creation of possibilities and options for further consideration. To keep from missing good ideas, you want a wide range of possibilities, including many that you will later discard. Such imagination tends to be impeded by traditional thinking and sound judgment.

For example: take out a sheet of paper. Write the name of the single best person to be honored for making a contribution to the world. Before you write down your answer, imagine that others may later be looking over your shoulder, and that you will be judged by the quality of your choice.

Alternatively, jot down the names of twenty or so people who *might* be good candidates. Include those that other people — perhaps a musician, a civil rights worker, a judge, a business executive, a medical doctor, or a religious leader — might include. Your task is now to come up with a good list for further consideration.

Which process leaves you feeling stuck? Which would help you find a surprising, instructive nominee?

The brainstorming of vacation plans, to use another example, will be far more creative if you are asked to nominate some possibilities rather than to suggest the single place where you would most like to go for a vacation next year.

One benefit of generating ideas first and evaluating them later is that it makes it easier to come up with unprecedented ideas. Even when thinking alone, we often hesitate to formulate an idea that others might criticize or ridicule. When generating ideas is a separate activity it is easier to loosen up and create a broad spectrum of possible options — to be evaluated later. Knowing that there will be a chance to evaluate makes it easier to hold judgment in check while brainstorming is under way. Having people think privately even for a minute or so increases the number of ideas, increases participation, and reduces the risk that the idea first mentioned — the one that had the least thought behind it — will get the most discussion.

A few years back a freight railroad ran into serious financial troubles. Desperate for ways to improve performance, management invited union representatives to a retreat at which they tried to agree on new policies that would rescue the company.

One issue they discussed involved a contract provision called "Meals and Rest," which had been a subject of intense conflict every time the contract was renegotiated. The railroad ran big loads of raw materials and industrial products across the vast empty plains of North America. Decades before, the union had won the right to stop the train in a town and get out for a hot meal — which took on special significance in the winter when work on the trains was cold, and the engineers knew that the management dining room was staffed with fine French chefs. Management worried that the delay in delivering the load, the cost of keeping rolling stock idle, and the uncertainty over whether employees would stop or not, put the railroad at a serious disadvantage against competitors who worked without the provision.

They agreed to use a brainstorming procedure to come up with some new ideas. The first idea was suggested by a union rep, that the company could pay workers to go without a meal. The managers protested loudly, but the facilitator, a union man, reminded them that no criticism was allowed during the first phase of generating ideas. Then one of the management team suggested calling ahead to a restaurant and having someone from the restaurant meet the train with a meal in a basket. A former engineer said, "I can do better than that. It takes an awful long time to slow a mile-long train down and start it up again. Why not hang the basket on a hook and grab it as the train goes by? We used to do that with mailbags in the old days." Everyone agreed that that was a fine manly way for an engineer to get his dinner. Then the secretary who had been keeping the minutes piped up. "These locomotives put out a lot of electrical power, right? Enough to run a microwave oven? That should get them a hot meal." In the years of considering only two options — continue the practice of "Meals and Rest" or eliminate it, everyone had missed the invention of a new technology that could meet everyone's interests.

Nominate a number of options and flesh them out so that you have a better idea of which makes the most sense. Then you can improve ideas that seem promising. Discovering difficulties with one idea, you might discard it and move on to others. As you evaluate and weigh the results of brainstorming, you still don't have to tie yourself down. Just note the good and bad points of options and compare them with one another.

A third distinct form of thinking is to make a decision. Deciding is making some kind of commitment, if only to yourself. "I have decided to turn down that job." "We have decided that this summer we will take our vacation in the mountains." "I have decided that Jones is the best person for that job, and she is the one I am going to support."

Deciding is far easier when it comes as part of a systematic approach. Instead of having to judge an idea against a universe of unknown possibilities, you merely have to look at the options you created and pick the one that seems best. Rather than weigh a specific idea against unknown competitors, you can choose among known quantities. Deciding is also easier if you know that you will have a chance to revisit the decision after some experience.

DO NEXT: TURN GOOD IDEAS INTO OPERATIONAL PLANS

Good thinking often goes nowhere. Making good decisions is not the same as implementing them. Alan's one-time employer and mentor Ralph Coverdale used to point out, "I can stay in bed all day having decided to get up." Many people who are brilliant creative thinkers don't make things happen because they omit the step of turning big ideas into operational plans. In the words of the old adage, "The road to hell is paved with good intentions." You need to turn big ideas into next steps — something to do now.

Make ideas operational. The desired product of thinking in Quadrant IV is a set of suggestions that are sufficiently detailed so that you know what to do. *Getting to YES* pointed out advantages of making a proposal "yes-able" — one that it is easy for another to accept. In Quadrant IV you want to turn a suggested strategy into plans that are "doable." A doable plan is a set of instructions that are sufficiently clear to ensure they are carried out without further questions and produce the desired result.

SECOND, CLARIFY A VISION OF JOINTLY USING THIS SKILL: WE ALL "THINK IN SYNC," SYSTEMATICALLY

PROBLEM: THE MORE PEOPLE, THE WORSE THE IMPACT OF DISORGANIZED THINKING

If you live alone and keep a sloppy house, you are likely to be less efficient at getting things done around the house. Still, you know reasonably well how to navigate through the mess. You know which of the piles on the floor is the most promising place to search for your favorite shirt, and where you left the remote control. If you live with someone else, and you are both sloppy, the problem is worse. Each of you leaves things in the other's way. Your roommate tries to clean up, and puts things away where you won't find them for weeks. When you work by yourself, chaotic thinking is an obstacle. When you work with others, it can be a catastrophe. Disorganization snowballs.

We All Think Haphazardly — Differently

If we all thought unsystematically in just the same way, then thinking with more people would not make the disorganization worse. But we all have different habits or patterns of thought. Usually these patterns don't mesh. While others try to understand what is going wrong, one person wants to jump ahead to a solution. We point out defects in each other's bright idea, instead of trying to build on it. We are typically unclear about what collective thinking is supposed to produce. We suffer from distraction. Even two find it difficult to coordinate their thinking. With larger numbers, thinking that bounces around at random produces random results. Any meeting can become a "bull session." Instead of helping, we get in each other's way.

VISION: WE ARE ALL USING THE SAME SIMPLE PATTERN TO ORGANIZE OUR JOINT THINKING

Two heads are not better than one when they get in each other's way. Systematic thinking helps us to organize multiple heads to work effectively together. Each step in the process is enriched and enlightened by fresh ideas, different points of view, and the wisdom of different experiences.

With a framework like the Circle Chart in mind, you are doubly empowered. You can think systematically. And now you have a model of how to organize collective thinking. Whether you are collaborating with one person or with several, the Circle Chart provides a framework for any meeting. The goal is to "think in sync" through the four quadrants. And within its quadrants, a group can further refine its collective thinking by noting when it is brainstorming options, when it is evaluating them, and when it is trying to reach a decision.

Joint systematic thinking offers a group the same benefits it offers an individual. Additional virtues of systematic thinking appear when it is used in a group:

- The distraction of many voices will not lead us to skip a vital step in our reasoning. Instead, people are orchestrated into a unit that proceeds deliberately together.

- Joint systematic thinking provides a simple taxonomy that can be used to sort ideas for later use. When someone interjects a non sequitur, we don't have to choose between losing the idea on the table or losing the new thought. We have a place to put the new thought and assurance that the system will bring us back to it.

- Systematic thinking makes our reasoning explicit, so that it can be questioned and tested. This helps us avoid the peril of groupthink — when everyone in a group goes along with a bad idea, thinking that others surely thought it through carefully, or out of fear of seeming disloyal by questioning it.

- Instead of getting unanimity by crushing dissent, systematic thinking helps us identify *why* we disagree. Knowing exactly where our reasoning diverges helps us examine both strands and choose the better one. The Circle Chart elicits different viewpoints and provides a framework that makes it easier to choose among them.

Return to the example of the coworkers planning an office party. Even in that simple situation lurk all the pitfalls of disorganized thinking that make more important matters go astray. And groups thinking well together will display much the same behavior whether they are thinking about a simple party or the way to rescue a failing company. What would it look like if the same group of people were thinking in sync?

ANN: Okay, let's try to be quick so we can get back to work. Bill, could you be our recorder and put this on the whiteboard?

BILL: Sure.

ANN: Let's start by hearing about some Quadrant I data from last year's party that we should consider. Here's one to get us started. I saw a lot of people leave early. The party started at five and by six-thirty half of us were gone. Does that match up with what you saw?

BILL: Yes. What caused that? Did we run out of drinks or something?

CHRIS: I was talking with Samantha in accounting, but she left early because she had to meet her husband.

DALE: I heard a few people say that they wanted to bring their boyfriends or wives or whatever.

ANN: If there were no spouses then who were all those people I didn't recognize?

CHRIS: They work here. Some were people I had been introduced to but I couldn't remember their names. It was pretty embarrassing.

BILL: Hold on while I write this up. "Didn't . . . know . . . names." Okay.

DALE: We didn't run out of liquor. If anything, we had too much. Dan Jenkins got awfully drunk.

ANN: Why do you say that?

DALE: He was slurring his speech and having trouble walking straight.

ANN: Sounds convincing. Was there anyone else who drank too much?

CHRIS: Not that I saw.

BILL: Okay. Let's get some more stuff in Quadrant I. What else? Other problems?

CHRIS: It shouldn't be called a Christmas party because of our Jewish colleagues.

ANN: Oh come on. You're being too sensitive.

CHRIS: No I'm not. This is important.

BILL: Let's figure out why we're disagreeing. I'll write Chris's suggestion down as a Quadrant III prescription. It sounds plausible, but we're not committing to anything yet without thinking it through. What would go in the other quadrants to lead up to it? I guess the diagnosis is that someone will feel left out if the office function has a religious name and they aren't part of that religion, right?

CHRIS: Of course.

BILL: How about the data? Did you hear anyone say that they were offended?

CHRIS: Not really.

DALE: But we don't know they weren't offended. I don't think we have data either way.

BILL: We can ask around to check on that. Assuming for the moment that Chris is right, any specific suggestions for Quadrant IV about a name change?

CHRIS: How about holiday party?

BILL: We don't have to call it anything. No name.

ANN: Year-end party?

BILL: I like "year-end party." We could say that we are cele-
brating a successful year for the firm, make it a reward
for good work.

ANN: Any objections? All right. Let's tentatively say "year-
end party." We could send it around and ask if anyone
objects. Let's look back at the symptoms. Someone got
drunk. Why was that? Does he always act that way, or
was there not enough food?

Etc. . . .

As a group we need not follow the four quadrants in lock-
step, start to finish. When confronting several issues, we can
list data for all of them, then move on to diagnoses and so on.
We could pick off one problem at a time and run it through to
plausible steps to "do next." We can start with a prescription
and check backward for a diagnosis and data that support it.
Or we can combine all these approaches. The important thing
is that for every issue we articulate our thinking in each quadrant — or identify where we have blank spaces that need to be
filled.

The following page depicts the recording on the board at
this stage of the meeting. A good goal in recording systematic thinking is to create a record that anyone walking into
the meeting in the middle would be able to read and understand the group's thinking so far. The chief benefit, however,
is not for late arrivals. Each of us can check what we have
accomplished and get ourselves back on track when we have
been distracted by private thoughts or the hubbub of many
voices.

Thinking in sync will not lead everyone to have the same
ideas, or even to agree. It will help us understand where we

I DATA	II DIAGNOSIS	III DIRECTION	IV DO NEXT
Many left early	Not enough snacks?	Invite spouses?	Holiday party?
	Had to meet spouses?		No name?
			<u>Year-end party</u>
<u>Embarrassed</u>	<u>Didn't know names</u>		
At least one person drank too much			
No data yet	Some offended by particular religious name for party?	Change name to be more inclusive	

disagree and why — a crucial first step toward coming to a consensus about what to do. It should help our discussions go more quickly, the way that traffic lights help cars move through a busy intersection.

THEN LEAD: STIMULATE OTHERS
TO THINK SYSTEMATICALLY

As part of a group working on a problem, you can keep two parallel purposes in mind. One is to help us do a good job on the problem at hand. The other is to improve the quality of our collective thinking in the future. Your vision of good systematic thinking can serve as the goal toward which you gently guide your colleagues. The challenge is great. If you succeed the benefits will be great as well.

Consider this example:

A few decades ago, a small British company became one of the first firms to mass manufacture ceramic electronics components. The company built its reputation in the industry for adhering to the highest quality standards, taking great care over the precise mix of materials, the temperature of the ovens, and the time needed for heating. For years it followed the same procedures and prospered.

Suddenly, in the space of a few months, the company hit hard times. Orders from clients plummeted. The management frantically tried to figure out what was going wrong. One meeting went something like this:

MANAGING DIRECTOR: I've been worried that this was going to happen. Sooner or later the production staff was going to get lazy about obeying the manufacturing protocols. We need to devote more resources to make sure that we adhere to the manufacturing standards.

PRODUCTION MANAGER: All right, I'll try, but . . . well, I think we need to consider whether our price is the problem, though. We have a very highly paid workforce.

FINANCE DIRECTOR: I agree. I think we were too generous with the union. Can we renegotiate the agreement?

MANAGING DIRECTOR: It's a three-year agreement. We don't have that long.

MARKETING DIRECTOR: With all due respect, the problem is not production. Other companies have bigger marketing budgets. They have more salesmen to send to the clients. That's why they're taking our business. We need to increase our marketing staff.

CHIEF ENGINEER: Maybe we shouldn't be investing more in this industry if the margins are dropping. We should salvage what we can and expand into other areas. This technology is on the way out. The customers are probably switching over to other kinds of components. We should reconfigure for different products.

MANAGING DIRECTOR: I have heard your views, and now I want you to support my decision. We're going to let our products win back the market for us the way we always have, by having the tightest production standards in the business. I want a plan on my desk Monday next for how we are going to improve the rigor of our production operations.

Imagine that you are an assistant working with the chief engineer, and that your boss took you along to the meeting. How might you try to make the group's thinking work better? Put down the book for a moment and think. What might you say?

It's Hard to Get Others to Think About Thinking
Getting others to change their habits is always difficult. Persuading colleagues to adopt new procedures for thinking

together has special challenges. The resistance caused by telling people what to do is especially acute when the quality of their thinking is at issue. "Your thinking could be improved" sounds too much like "You're stupid" or "You're crazy."

Further, when people are confronted with a substantive problem, it is likely to absorb their attention. It is difficult to get them to step back and examine the *way* they are approaching the problem, rather than the problem itself. Worse, the circular nature of thinking about thinking can tie you in knots. Trying to get people to think together about the way they think together is bound to be confusing. Imagine you tried to intervene in the electronics company meeting by prompting your superiors to examine their thinking methods:

MARKETING DIRECTOR: . . . that's why they're taking our business. We need to increase our marketing staff.

YOU: With all due respect, we're thinking chaotically here. What we need to do is to think systematically from data to diagnosis to dir —

MANAGING DIRECTOR: What the hell are you talking about?

YOU: Well, sir, I mean to say that the first problem is the *way* we're thinking about the lost sales. We're just bouncing from one idea to another without thoroughly exploring any of them. Look, let's think systematically about our thinking process. What data do you observe about the way we're talking about the data of the substantive problem?

CHIEF ENGINEER: What on earth do you mean? Have you been taking some management course?

YOU: We need to diagnose the problem before we decide what to do.

FINANCE DIRECTOR: Getting back to the question of the union wage scale . . .

It is difficult to convince your colleagues with abstract theories. And sharing data about the way we are talking is difficult.

Think Systematically Yourself

Rather than try to lead an impromptu seminar on systematic thinking, try to figure out what you should do yourself. Start with the simplest diagnosis: your colleagues aren't familiar with any organized way of thinking and don't know the benefits it could bring. Some possible strategies for dealing with that diagnosis are:

- We might receive organized training in systematic thinking.
- The boss might give people a book on systematic thinking and tell them to read it.
- A superior might issue a clear directive telling all subordinates to think systematically.

Or:

- During our discussions someone might interject a question or a comment to stimulate a particular step in systematic thinking about a real issue as we deal with it.

Since this last strategy is one that you can attempt yourself, without depending on anyone else, it is a good place to start.

Stimulate Joint Use of the Tools

The easiest way to introduce a group to systematic thinking is to steer an orderly discussion of a problem they are trying to tackle. Systematic thinking is so useful that most people quickly see its benefits.

Once a young legal academic was invited to discuss problems in the Boston Housing Court with a group of public interest attorneys. He simply guided them through a Circle

Chart analysis of the problem, and they devised a plan to petition the legislature for specific changes. At the end of the meeting, the chairwoman said, "Thanks for your help on the housing court issue. By the way, do you have any written material on that chart you used?"

If you limit yourself to asking relevant questions in a systematic way, your position in the hierarchy can become an advantage instead of a handicap. You might not have the rank to tell others what to do, but surely you are allowed to try to learn something from the older and wiser heads around you.

Ask for data. If you think that your colleagues are not collecting important data about the situation, ask them to fill you in on the facts.

MARKETING DIRECTOR: . . . that's why they're taking our business. We need to increase our marketing staff.

YOU: Excuse me, I'm afraid I don't have enough experience to follow what you have been saying. What exactly have the customers said about why they aren't ordering from us anymore?

MANAGING DIRECTOR: Well? Who's talked to them?

MARKETING DIRECTOR: I'll call my friends at some of the clients as soon as we get done here.

YOU: I am curious whether they are still buying our sort of electrodes, and if so, from whom.

MARKETING DIRECTOR: Yes. If they are getting them elsewhere we need to know how much. They may be paying less for their labor costs than we are.

YOU: Is there anything else we need to know that I could try to find out?

Ask for diagnosis. If you ask others to educate you, you don't even implicitly criticize them for not knowing the answers. And by volunteering to find out more, you offer part of the solution instead of merely a problem. You want to be sure that others won't dismiss a good question simply because it may be difficult to find the answers. It is equally easy to prod others to diagnose a problem instead of jumping to a solution.

MARKETING DIRECTOR: Well, I called Ian Sturrock up in Glasgow and he told me that they started getting their electrodes for less from an American company.

YOU: I don't understand how they could be charging less. What could they be doing differently?

FINANCE DIRECTOR: They must be charging less for labor. We have to go back to the union and ask for concessions . . .

YOU: That *is* a plausible explanation. It might not be the only one. I suppose they might be doing something else differently.

FINANCE DIRECTOR: Like what?

YOU: I don't know. How much less are they charging?

MARKETING DIRECTOR: Less than 50 percent of our price.

PRODUCTION DIRECTOR: Our labor costs are only about 35 percent of the price of the product.

FINANCE DIRECTOR: Maybe they get their supplies cheaper.

PRODUCTION DIRECTOR: What if they have found a cheaper way to control product quality?

You don't have to offer an answer yourself to raise the issue.

Diagnosis is a crucial step. In the actual situation, the company found on further investigation that the American competitor did not demand nearly as tight control over the manufacturing process, allowing them to run their assembly plant much more cheaply. Customers found that the electrodes they made worked just as well.

In many cases, an accurate diagnosis points us straight at a better approach. The company decided to spend less on controlling the manufacturing process. There are still a lot of questions. Turning ideas into practical next steps is perhaps the single most critical aspect of producing change. People meet, discuss, brainstorm, and evaluate the ideas they generate but often leave a meeting without a clear idea of when the next meeting will be, what should be done before that meeting, and who is going to do it. Which can we safely spend less on: monitoring the exact temperature? the cost of materials?

It may be that once the crisis is solved, you can encourage others to think about how this problem happened in the first place. Again, all you need do is ask questions. What went wrong with our thinking that we invested far more than would be helpful in production standards? Why didn't we make wiser choices from the beginning?

One way both to help a group think systematically about an immediate problem on which it is working and to begin to spread the advantages of systematic thinking is to offer a few key headings on a whiteboard while asking a question about next steps. For example:

DATA	DIAGNOSIS	DIRECTION	DO NEXT
(Symptoms)	(Possible causes)	(Possible approaches)	(Next steps)

"Before this meeting breaks up, what are some things that we should look into before we meet again?

Orderly thinking is a great help. It can help you with your own work. It can also help you improve joint work when working with others, both as a vision of collaborative thinking toward which to work and as a guideline on how best to help achieve that vision.

5 LEARNING

INTEGRATE THINKING WITH DOING

No amount of thinking is enough. You can improve your ability to think, but however systematic or well directed, it will not be perfect. When we think, we create simplified representations of the world — so that we can understand it better or imagine a new reality. Those simple representations will be incomplete. There are always important things you don't know — and there is no way of predicting where the gaps in your understanding will be. You can't know how much you don't know.

Therefore, there is always a need to learn more. You need to test your thinking. You need to compare your predictions with what happens. It is not a question of finding out whether the thinking is flawed — you can be confident that it is — but how. If you want to get things done you need to learn more about the task you are going to work on. The third essential element in getting things done is LEARNING — improving your thinking by testing it out in action. The basic skill is to integrate thinking with doing.

Why is it difficult? The learning you need to do at work is not like the learning most of us had to do in school. In school we learn facts, formulas, and theories. For the most part we don't learn how to *do* things. And learning how to do things is quite different from learning *about* things. Further, for most of us education consisted of learning, or at best re-creating, things that other people already knew. Unless they reach the point of writing a Ph.D. dissertation, many students were never asked to find new answers to new problems.

To be able to help others improve their skill in jointly learning from our work, you first need to develop the habit of learning from what you do, even when you are doing it alone. Getting better at learning starts with understanding what is holding you back now.

FIRST, DEVELOP A PERSONAL SKILL: KEEP LEARNING FROM WHAT YOU DO

PROBLEM: PLANS ARE BASED ON MISTAKEN ASSUMPTIONS, ACTIONS ON MISTAKEN PLANS

Just as sometimes people act without sufficient systematic thinking, so there are times when they think without sufficient action. There are times when we become concerned that plans should be "right" before starting to work on them. Authors have a tendency to keep drafting and redrafting an outline before grinding out the text. (As we write a book on getting things done, we risk writing pages of advice before we personally try to put that advice into practice.) We all tend to keep gathering information and generating ideas long after we have good ideas to try. Or we speculate about the merits of two different courses of action far longer than it would take to try out both.

When you feel ready to take action, it may be too late. Someone else has already published a similar book. The shares have gone up — or down; the property has been sold; the position has been filled.

The worst aspect of delaying action is not missing an opportunity. Delaying action hurts the quality of the work, because there is no chance to learn how to improve it before the job is done. Sometimes we base our plans on factual assumptions, only to find that they were mistaken. Even though the chance is not lost altogether, all the work up to that point is wasted.

A refugee from Europe came to the United States in 1947. He had been a wealthy industrialist, and wanted to use the fragment of his fortune that remained to start a new business to leave to his children. An expert on industrial materials, he decided to develop a new form of glue that could be used where other glues were useless. After years of work he developed one with the characteristics he wanted. It was easy to handle, quick-drying, waterproof, and resistant to electricity. Once he created the formula he went right into mass production and quickly began selling large amounts of the glue. It was months later before he heard the first reports of problems. The glue had every good quality except stickiness.

What is the reason that we so often find it hard to get into action, or find ourselves in trouble once we do?

CAUSE: YOU SEGREGATE THINKING FROM DOING

One underlying cause is that we disconnect thinking about a problem from doing something about it. Frequently planning is compartmentalized away from implementation — in time, place, or the people involved. We think until the planning is finished, and then work until the job is done. The quality of both thinking and doing suffers.

Thinking needs to be refreshed with data gathered in action. Action needs to be constantly redirected by fresh thinking. The return on either activity diminishes the longer they continue apart. Each successive hour that one thinks without testing will be less productive than the previous one.

You Postpone Action Until Plans Are Polished

Concerned about the risk of getting something "wrong," we put off doing things until plans are perfect. Since there is a risk in actually doing something, we postpone that risk as long as possible.

To some extent our training is at fault. Most education, from elementary school through business school, is devoted to working on discrete intellectual problems. The teacher knows the answer and the student is supposed to figure it out. For such "closed" problems there is only one solution, and we are taught to keep working until we find it. The goal is to get it right, to get a perfect score, a 100 on the exam.

Most of life is not like that. The challenges we face are open-ended — problems like those of air pollution, safety, education, efficient production, and managing human resources — problems to which there are no perfect answers. The need is to get something done to improve the situation, to make some progress. Yet, trained as we are, we want plans to be the best possible. We work on and on, seeking to "solve" an open problem by producing better and better plans — yet not actually *doing* anything.

Perseverance is a virtue — when the goal has been well chosen. The goal of planning, however, is not high-quality plans but high-quality work. And that will not be achieved by endless planning.

Once Work Starts, You Ignore Ways to Improve

Experience is a good teacher, but only for those who take the time to learn. Too often, once we start to work on a task, we adopt a "can do" approach and barge ahead. While working we fail to observe ourselves and avoid thinking about how the task might be done better.

You fail to consider mid-course corrections. Once you have become well engaged in a task you know far more about it than you did before you began. Yet we all tend to follow a blueprint that was prepared when we knew less. We sometimes treat plans as sacred, and carry them out to the letter, even though we made them ourselves. For example, I decide to make the trip to my vacation home on Sunday because it is the only day I can get a ferry reservation for my car. My daughter asks if she can borrow the car that weekend. I agree, thinking that I don't really need the car at the beach. I still wait until Sunday to take the bus, wasting half the weekend, simply because I had already decided that Sunday was the day to go.

It seems easier to follow a set path than to stop and chart a new course. And perhaps it is, for the moment. In the long run, though, you would probably get to your destination more quickly — or even to a better destination — if you took the time to check the plans against changed circumstances.

When the plans have been produced by others we are even less likely to question them. One benefit is that if the plans don't work well, it's somebody else's fault. Roger once watched in horror as a contractor cut down a magnificent oak. The contractor didn't want to ask the architect to change the proposed location of a house by a few feet, even though the architect hadn't known of the tree's location. People tend to act like members of the famous Light Brigade . . .

> *Theirs not to make reply,*
> *Theirs not to reason why,*
> *Theirs but to do and die . . .*

In some organizations a "mandate" is taken as a substitute for thought, including common sense: "That's not what my mandate tells me, so I am not going to do it that way."

No revision of plans in the light of new information will take place, however, unless you observe what is going on and compare it to what you expected. Too often we fail to learn in the famous "school of trial and error" in time to apply its lessons to the task in which we are engaged.

You fail to learn for the future. Sometimes you cannot learn a lesson in time to apply it right away. You thought the eggs were safe all in one basket, but they got smashed. You forgot to consult, and sold furniture the children wanted. You thought the client would like your presentation, but he hated it. It happens all the time.

You can't undo the past. You can learn from it. You can do something different with the next basket of eggs. Too often, instead of learning for the future we let bygones be bygones.

Review usually gets a low priority. Any benefits of review are off somewhere in the future, other items are pressing here and now. When newspaper reporters meet a deadline and publish a story, they start looking forward to the next deadline. Like the rest of us, they rarely have an interest in reviewing the methods they used to see what they might want to do differently.

When we do set aside time for review, we often fail to use that time productively. Review becomes an opportunity for meting out blame (and sometimes praise) rather than for planning improvements. Alan was hired to consult with a successful professional sports team that had fallen on hard times. He noticed that the players were unenthusiastic about holding their team meeting after a game. When asked why, they said that after a victory they expected a perfunctory meeting that mainly wasted time. After a loss, the manager berated those he thought responsible.

Of course, congratulating people for hard work can be useful. It can give them the satisfaction that keeps them willing to make sacrifices. It will not, however, improve their skills or generate ideas to improve their future performance. If you think of times when you learned the most in school, it was probably not when you got your report card. Likely, you benefited more when a teacher took you aside to suggest changes in a paper or an experiment. You may not have a full-time teacher anymore, but you can still concentrate on learning instead of punishing or rewarding yourself.

AIM: INTEGRATE THINKING AND DOING

If you want to learn more from experience, and thus get more done, what do you need to do?

The first step is to reconsider the usual choice between spending time thinking or acting. The tradeoff is illusory. Getting into action usually helps your thinking more than spending more time thinking.

Rather than treating thinking and doing as distinct activities that should be kept apart, it makes better sense to integrate thought and action. Harness action closely in the service of clear, rigorous thought. Enrich that systematic thinking by systematically injecting fresh hard data. Such data comes from observing what happens when we try out ideas in the real world.

Imagine that the manager of a ski equipment store is troubled by the long time it takes her staff to get a customer fitted with the right equipment and through the line at the register. If she devotes an hour to rigorous systematic thinking she should come up with some ideas. If she keeps thinking for ten hours, she may come up with more ideas, but probably not ten times more. And if she thought for an hour, tried out some of her ideas for an hour, and then spent an hour improving her first plans or inventing new ones, she will have better ideas at the end of three hours of combined thinking and doing than she would after ten hours of pure thinking.

Jump into Action Early

It is useful to do at least a little planning. Successful preparation will provide a foundation for repeating what works, and for improving what doesn't. A great chef can create a delicious new meal. However, if he fails to record the recipe, he may not be able to re-create his success a few weeks later. For more complex jobs, good preparation will include a written scheme of what you are going to do, and some hypotheses about expected results. It may include a rough draft of further plans, and also suggest information to look out for as you proceed.

Still, plans will never be perfect. You can never *know* that there is not some course of action better than the one you picked. You could always wait and do more research. There are always more people who might have advice. You need to decide: shall I continue the planning process or shall I start doing something? Since you know that we all tend to wait and wait until plans are perfect, good general advice is "Don't wait." Don't think of action as a single stage of activity at the end of which there is a final product. As you approach any task you want to look for early opportunities to test assumptions, to try out ideas, to test plans.

Don't choose between planning and doing. The wisest course is usually not to choose between more planning and starting work. It is to do both. Getting started does not mean that planning has to stop. The relationship between plans and action should be a two-way exchange in which each benefits from the other. In most situations the benefits of getting started will outweigh the benefits of further delay while plans are being polished. One of the best ways to improve plans is to try them out, at least in a small way. Pilot projects, test borings, trial runs, and work with models and simulations are all ways of starting to act in time to have later versions of a plan benefit from what has been learned in the field.

Ask: what's the risk? When you hesitate because of the perceived risk of trying out what you have in mind, ask yourself, "How does that compare with the risk of doing nothing — of leaving matters as they are?"

The personnel manager of a large electronics company considered removing a payment-by-results scheme. As often happens with such schemes, the employees had figured out how to manipulate the amount of bonus they received without actually producing more. Nevertheless, he was reluctant to see the scheme replaced with a flat day rate. No matter how unsatisfactory the present scheme, he feared that the workers would slack off and produce less if the scheme were removed.

Then the personnel manager asked himself what would happen if nothing was changed. Based on the last few years' experience, payments would continue to rise without any increase in production. He figured that the risk of continuing was greater than that of experimenting with a new system. He decided to make the change and test the result. He could always change back.

In some circumstances you cannot afford for plans to be anything but perfect and foolproof before taking even the first step. After all, you do not want to jump out of an airplane with a parachute unless you are sure that the preparation has been as good as possible. Yet, even here, some "action" started a long way back. Rather than spend endless hours at a desk until plans for a perfect parachute had been completed, wise people took some preliminary drawings, built a few model parachutes, and tried them out with weights dropped from bridges and towers. Musical producers do a trial run off Broadway.

Most of the ideas in this book were developed in just this way. And we keep improving them. Before publishing this book we began teaching workshops for professionals based on the ideas, testing whether hardworking practitioners actually found them useful. Changes were made. Getting started is bound to produce information that could make the next version of plans better than the last.

Start Reviewing Almost Immediately

Just as you should not hesitate to leave off thinking and get your hands dirty, you should be quick to put down tools and think about what you are doing and how. It is tempting to assume that the proper time for review is when a task is completed. Students are graded at the end of a course. Investment bankers gather to assess their performance after a big merger is finished. But the truth is that frequent reviews are more useful. Whether or not you are making good progress, you can stop and review your methods and improve them. Why wait?

One would expect that after you have finished doing something, you could devise a better approach than you could before starting. Yet we often forget that you could also devise a better approach after you are half-finished. Where possible, it is wise to benefit immediately from wisdom that can be garnered from reviewing your own performance.

Once you get into action, your attention is absorbed by the minutiae of the task. It is easy to lose sight of the big picture. You may become so involved in some intricate aspect of what you are doing that you spend more time on that issue than it deserves. While working on this book Alan took a break to fix a problem with his car. After trying for half an hour to manipulate a cotter pin into a small hole in an awkward position in the engine he remarked, "I would have done better to have stepped back and thought for a bit after the first five minutes!"

You may find it useful to prepare a simple list of questions that would help structure a review. The following questions are suggestive:

An Illustrative Short Checklist for Review

WW? What seems to have **W**orked **W**ell?
DD? What might I want to **D**o **D**ifferently?
What guidelines does this suggest?
For work in progress?
For future work?

A review is more likely to be productive if it happens when the data is still fresh in your mind. If you pause to review while a task is still under way, review will get the attention it deserves, because conclusions are likely to have immediate relevance. Once a task is completed we are inclined to treat it as a closed book and move on to something else.

The authors of this book teach a five-day negotiation workshop at Harvard Law School to practicing lawyers and other professionals. The teaching staff includes young academics and students who facilitate discussions among small groups of participants. The teaching staff pay enormous attention to each evening's review, because they are eager to improve their performance for the next day. On Friday afternoon, by contrast, they are restless, wanting to get the review over with as soon as possible and go out for a beer. The greater part of their learning comes from the mid-course reviews.

There is a tension between accomplishing this job as planned and devoting time to thinking about better ways to do it. Balance is required. Few individuals — and even fewer groups — get the balance right. Most should spend more time in reviewing and improving their performance.

Experience can be a powerful teacher, but it doesn't work alone. It is said that medicine made few advances until doctors began to conduct autopsies and discovered when their diagnoses had been correct and when their patients had really died of something else. You are better off if you do not bury your mistakes — or your successes. Review your completed projects both to hand out praise and — more important — to learn how to do better in the future.

Follow short cycles of PREPARE — ACT — REVIEW. To keep your thinking and action integrated and balanced, you can follow a simple pattern:

PREPARE → ACT → REVIEW → PREPARE . . .

and repeat it again and again in the course of your work.

We can expand the Circle Chart from the last chapter. Taken alone, the Circle Chart is an exercise in pure thinking, with no action taken. Since it ends where it started, it does not convey a sense of forward progress. Rather than going around and around within it, as soon as you see how to move forward, dive into the world of action. This is suggested graphically in the Sine Curve Chart on page 124. The field of action is below the wavy line. Below that line we implement plans, try out ideas, do actual work: manufacture cars, treat patients, harvest crops, make deals. Everything above the wavy line is thinking. We think about the work we do: diagnose causes of difficulty, hold planning meetings, review performance, suggest mid-course corrections, prepare revised plans.

BEYOND THE CIRCLE CHART: A SINE CURVE

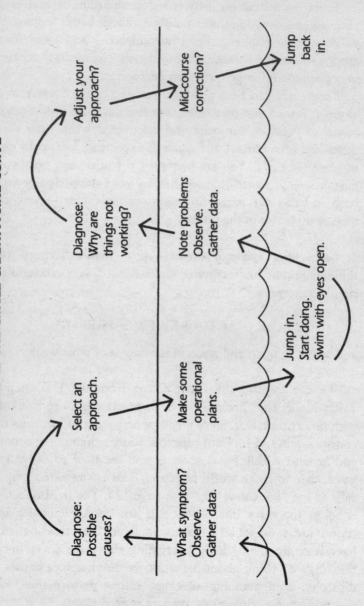

Diagnose: Possible causes?

Select an approach.

Diagnose: Why are things not working?

Adjust your approach?

What symptom? Observe. Gather data.

Make some operational plans.

Note problems Observe. Gather data.

Mid-course correction?

Jump in. Start doing. Swim with eyes open.

Jump back in.

The chart shows that as you follow the sine curve you are continually diving into the "sea" of activity (but swimming with your eyes open), and then resurfacing into the "sunlight" of thought — all the while moving constantly toward your goals.

Repeat the cycle over and over. After every review, prepare for what to do next.

Every review provides fresh information leading to new things to be done, new plans to be made and implemented.

Preparation, action, and review — even if done only once — are essential stages in learning from any task. The sequence is most powerful when used in repeated cycles. Repeating the process:

Avoids paralysis at decision points.

Working in short cycles liberates you from the need to get things right the first time. Knowing that you will revise your plans during the course of the work reduces the risk of getting stuck.

Allows quick integration of new information.

You are unlikely to stray far in the wrong direction if you regularly look up and see if you are getting closer to the objective.

Keeps effort focused where it will be most productive, instead of running into diminishing returns.

You don't have to waste time striving for perfection. That confidence lets you get going and start making progress sooner.

SECOND, CLARIFY A VISION OF JOINTLY USING THIS SKILL: PREPARE AND REVIEW TOGETHER

PROBLEM: THE MORE PEOPLE, THE GREATER THE DIFFICULTY OF LEARNING FROM EXPERIENCE

"Sunshine Software"

During the summer of 1996 the operations committee of a major U.S. software company worked hard and produced a company-wide plan for 1997. The plan identified which products were going to be discontinued, revised, or supported with special marketing budgets. The plan was approved by top management and announced company-wide to all offices and branches throughout the world.

The operations committee consisted of able senior officers of the company who worked hard, yet other employees were dumbfounded by what they had produced. The Japanese office thought that the plan was badly out of step with their market. People in other branches also were unhappy. But orders were orders. Throughout the company honest and hardworking officers and staff divided their efforts among trying to make the plan work, straining to interpret the plan to fit reality on the ground as they knew it, and preparing justifications for why the plan would not work in their districts. One young marketing executive asked her supervisor, "What should we do about this?"

"Get used to it," he replied. "This kind of thing happens all the time."

Some Plan, Others Do

In any organization there are likely to be some people who concentrate on making plans and other people who are responsible for their implementation. The larger the organization, the greater the effective distance is going to be between planners and doers. The result is that those who make the plans often fail to receive data that would cause them to question their assumptions.

One group, say the production planning department, is told to prepare plans. On completion they submit them to a higher authority. Management makes a big decision to go forward with the plans. The plans are transferred to the "doers," say the various manufacturing sections. The thinkers keep thinking, and the doers keep doing, without either group learning from the other's experience. The doers, not knowing the thinking behind the plans, are unsure if and where they can safely make adjustments. And the planners never get a chance to revise their plans to adjust for some difficulty in implementation.

Some Want Plans Perfect, Others Want to Jump into Action

In any group there are always people who want more time to think and are reluctant to get into action until they are sure their plans will produce the "right answer." It usually takes only one or two people to delay a whole group. Similarly there are always some who want to "press on regardless," making it difficult to get others to stop and review.

Review Is Often Postponed Until Nobody Cares

Getting real things done is usually seen as far more important than pausing and talking about it. The result is that often no review is made while there is still time to make mid-course corrections. Further, review after a particular project is completed is often put off until it has to be written up for a project report or, worse, for the annual report. By that time the project is gone like water over a dam and holds little interest. Review at this stage is rarely a joint effort. Someone is assigned to write up the report. The purpose of the report is rarely to learn from experience and develop guidelines for the future. A more likely purpose is to make performance look good. Such review is rarely an educational experience for the group.

We Rarely Review How We Are Collaborating

When we do stop to review a project we are likely to focus our attention on the substantive work. We are less likely to review the way in which we have been working together, or work on improving our cooperation. Unless we pay special attention, we will not consider what caused us to get out of step with one another and what we might learn from that experience. And if there are problems with our methods of working together, then finding better substantive approaches will not keep us from repeating mistakes next time. Problems in our substantive work often have their roots in the way we work together.

If the software firm does not address the lack of information sharing between the branch offices and the planning committee, then fixing the substance of the plan will do little good. A substantive review might lead them to figure out which products will do well in Japan this year. But it will not fix the approach that led to the mistake. They will likely run into the same problem next year with a different office.

There always seem to be more important things to do than to plan ways of improving our collaboration. Yet as the boss of a large chemical manufacturing site remarked, "We have learned that time spent in considering *how* we are working together, *how* we are reaching decisions, and planning ways of improving our cooperation is time that pays for itself in sheer gold."

VISION: EVERYONE HELPS INTEGRATE THINKING AND DOING

The same practices that help you do a better job will help the entire organization if applied on a company-wide scale. One goal for the future is that everyone in the organization will understand the value of starting to do things before plans have been polished, and of pausing promptly to see how things are going and how well we are working together. Anyone feels free to suggest that we start some aspect of the job in order to learn something. Anyone feels free to propose a pause for joint review. And we learn from experience together, so that we all get the benefit of what others learn.

We Prepare, Act, and Review the Way We Handle the Task

We are working to accomplish some substantive task. A primary purpose of observing and reviewing how we are working on a task is to learn how we might get that substantive task accomplished sooner or better.

Boeing's engineers had a rough time designing and building the first 737s. After a thorough review, they were able to fill a large volume with the record of the mistakes they made and blind alleys they traveled along the way. All the designers who later made the first 767s studied that book, and were able to produce their next aircraft far more quickly and effectively.

We Prepare, Act, and Review How We Work Together

We are also interested in learning from our actions how well we are collaborating. How well is that cooperation working? What guidelines might help us improve our working together, either on this task or on future ones? Among the goals of our joint review is to observe and learn how well we have been reviewing together. The vision is that we should be doing it routinely and well.

Of course, that is not the way it works in most government offices, most universities, or most companies. Once you become aware of the importance of learning from what you are doing when working alone, it is easier to be aware of it when collaborating with others. Unfortunately, when you look at how most groups integrate experience with thinking you will likely be dismayed.

Better Days at "Sunshine"

The company learned from the painful experience of the 1996 plan. The planning committee heard from some of the district managers how unhappy they were at being stuck with an unworkable plan without having any opportunity to affect the outcome. The committee scheduled a day to sit down and explore what had gone wrong. They looked at mistakes, but more importantly, at what in their approach had led them to make those mistakes.

When it came time to prepare the 1998 plan, the operations committee prepared a "draft plan" — what they would have adopted if they had followed the procedure used the previous year. A large meeting was held of people from the company's offices around the world to consider and suggest revisions based on their experience. People worked hard in committees and subcommittees and in long evening sessions. By and large they worked happily, pleased at being consulted and given the opportunity to bring their experience to bear on the planning process. By improving the process used to write the plan, the company ended up making great progress in the substance of it as well. The plan was more flexible, allowing for differences in local markets, and arranged for coordination between offices with similar needs.

THEN LEAD: HELP YOUR COLLEAGUES
LEARN FROM EXPERIENCE

The first part of this chapter focused on what you can do to improve your own skill in integrating thought and action. The second was devoted to clarifying a vision of the cooperative situation toward which you can work — how a group can learn by going through repeated cycles of PREPARE — ACT — REVIEW. Now we turn to the question of how you might "lead" colleagues (and yourself) toward that vision. When trying to get things done with others, how might you use the techniques of lateral leadership to get us all integrating thought with action?

The planning committee at "Sunshine Software" changed its methods. They reviewed their performance, they designed new approaches and quickly tried them out, and they scheduled time to learn from their first attempt with the new system. But how did that happen? Who said what, to help that occur? Assume that you were an experienced staff person at one of the software company's branches. What might you have done to help the committee learn from its experience?

It is likely that the committee gave more consideration to the substance of the task — what products to concentrate on and how to promote them — than on the process — how they should go about making choices. There is probably more opportunity to make improvement there. Better still, by itself it will tend to produce better substantive results. If you can jump-start the habit of examining the way the group works and producing better habits, then the cycle of PREPARE — ACT — REVIEW will develop its own momentum.

Offer Data: Report on Collective Learning Failures

When the 1997 plan had been circulated, the operations committee had a need for honest data about how it was working and about the impact of the planning process on company employees. Observe what you can from your vantage point, and ASK others what they noticed. Perhaps people are simply unhappy about not being consulted.

As you privately ask questions of people you know, look for DATA that would call your assumptions into doubt. Look for what was good about the plan as well as what might better have been done differently. And look for views of others that will help you get beyond your biases.

Having gathered data, you can offer the information to someone who can make good use of it. Too often the upper tiers of management don't hear about troubling information because lower ranks fear that the messenger will be shot. Thus planners are kept apart from data that would help them learn to do better. One approach is to offer the data privately to one individual who can think about what to do with them without being put on the spot.

Dear _____,

I am writing to you in your role as a member of the planning committee. I want to share the information I have observed and collected from my colleagues about how the plan is working out in the field. You are in a better position than I am to make sense of this data, and to decide whether to present these observations to the rest of the committee. I hope it helps you figure out what, if anything, to change for next year.

The first thing I noticed was that . . .

If you send a memo of complaints to the whole committee, each person's choice would be something like, "Do I agree with this complaint and take sides against my friends on the committee, or do I defend the hard work we did and difficult choices we made?" It is not hard to predict that the committee members will be strongly tempted to circle their wagons and blame any problems on the branch office workers.

The benefit of this approach is that it offers a different choice to one committee member: "Do I transmit this information to my friends so that *we* can do something about this before the problem gets any worse? Since my friends and I on the committee will get credit for any improvement, I will be happy to use the data."

Offer a Diagnosis: We Aren't Helping Others Learn

The operations committee was obviously unaware of facts that made parts of the plan inappropriate. That ignorance may be more the fault of those in the field who knew and could have communicated those facts than the fault of committee members who were unaware of what it was of which they were unaware. To remedy that communication gap you might work at either end.

You can offer a diagnosis of the problem to colleagues in your office: "I think the reason they make up plans that don't fit our situation is that we don't tell them enough about our situation. Might that be part of the problem?" Or you could pass a similar diagnosis back to headquarters.

When it comes to diagnosing causes of difficulty or causes of success, look for those relating to the *process* by which the two plans were prepared.

Offer Direction: Suggest That Colleagues Share Their Experience

Another approach is to direct a suggestion to someone who is in a better position to affect the situation. Consider the marketing executive whose boss told her that nothing could be done about the committee's failure to account for the problems facing the local offices. What might she say to encourage him to take a less fatalistic approach?

BOSS: Get used to it, it happens all the time.

KIM: Sounds like you have had some experience with this kind of thing.

BOSS: Year after year. I used to complain about it, but they never paid any attention.

KIM: So telling them to change hasn't worked. Maybe there's another approach. There might be something we could change.

BOSS: What could we do?

KIM: They are making plans without taking account of our situation, right? Presumably that's because they don't know the facts about our situation. For them to be ignorant about our situation two things have to happen: they don't ask, and we don't tell them without being asked. Maybe we can't get them to change, but we could change what we're doing.

BOSS: How am I supposed to know what information they need?

KIM: Good question. I'm not entirely sure. One thing we could do is send the information that we think is important and then ask whether that was useful or not.

BOSS: They still wouldn't change because they would have to admit they made a mistake in the first place. They aren't going to do that.

KIM: I think you are right that they have an interest in not looking bad, and that they'll try to protect themselves. We could take that onus off them by saying, "This is important information, sorry we didn't get this information to you before." If we are the only office giving the information then we can take part of the responsibility and still look good.

BOSS: Maybe that would help. But why should I? They are on the planning committee. I shouldn't have to do their job.

KIM: Of course you don't have to. If you decide to do it, it would be because you think you are better off putting in some effort that might lead to a better planning process, so that you would have the resources to meet your customers' needs. I thought I owed it to you to come up with some options to suggest. You know better than I do what decision you want to take.

Whenever you offer direction you want to be clear that you are not telling the recipient what he has to do. Take the role of an adviser who lays out scenarios that the decision maker can choose among, much as cabinet officials offer options to their president.

Do Something

How about reviewing the regular reports from the field to headquarters to see if omitted information might explain why the operations committee was unaware of the factual situation on the ground with which their 1997 plan (and their draft of the 1998 plan) seemed out of step? You might volunteer to prepare a draft of such a report.

One final thing to keep in mind when trying to get colleagues to adopt better practices: your first efforts are likely to be unsuccessful. You will make mistakes. You may anger some colleague. In short, you will find that some things you tried did not WORK WELL. After a bad result, you may be tempted to give the task up as hopeless. A better approach is to apply the techniques for learning to your own efforts. Analyze exactly what you did and look for what went wrong. Find some things to DO DIFFERENTLY when you try again. With practice and review you will become more effective.

6 ENGAGEMENT

OFFER EVERYONE A CHALLENGING ROLE

As you look around the office, you notice that some of your colleagues are more energetic than others. "Such is human nature," you might say, "It's the old story of the ant and the grasshopper. Some people are hard workers, and others aren't. Nothing I can do about it." There is some truth to this view. Any coach would agree that some athletes hustle more than others. A shop foreman knows that some factory operators are more diligent, and a CEO, that some managers are more vigorous.

But there is more to it. Perhaps some people *are* more disposed toward hard work. However, you can also see that everyone is more lively at some times than at others. Under the right circumstances each of us is more productive.

Alan once sat in with the management team of a British brewery as they met to evaluate and improve the company's training program. The managing director was running the meeting, with little success. It went on and on, accomplishing little. When the managing director had to leave to attend his next meeting, he handed over the helm to the production director. The production director took charge, ran the meeting smoothly and effectively, and soon completed the task. It is tempting to congratulate the production director for the good job he did once he took charge. The real question is: if he knew what to do, why didn't he try to help sooner?

If we are honest, we have to admit that we all have plenty of experience at not helping. Surely there has been a time when you pushed your chair back and "checked out" of a meeting. If someone had asked you what the last speaker said you would have had no idea. You catch yourself staring out the window. Like most people, you have days or weeks when you shrug off commitment to a project.

Asking why you don't work harder — and what you could do about it — is a good start toward figuring out how you can encourage others to put more into common efforts.

FIRST, DEVELOP A PERSONAL SKILL: SHAPE YOUR JOB TO INCLUDE INTERESTING CHALLENGES

Getting your organization to work better starts with getting yourself to work better. Once you have improved your skills you know more about helping others do the same. You will have more credibility as someone who can improve others' motivation if your own is seen to be high.

DATA: AT TIMES YOU HOLD BACK

Of course, it would be nice if you always worked up to your potential. The organization would get more done. It would help build your reputation as competent and committed. But motivating yourself is as much of a challenge as motivating anyone else. Yet it can be done.

To become better at motivating yourself, start by examining what diminishes your commitment on those occasions when you feel disengaged.

DIAGNOSIS: THE WAY YOU FRAME YOUR JOB LIMITS YOUR EFFORTS

We each carry in our heads a "frame" or story that we tell ourselves about our jobs. Sketch a mental picture of yourself at work. If you were to put a caption under that picture, what would it say? That picture and its caption is your frame on your job. It is a description of what you do and, implicitly, what is within your power and what isn't. To some extent the frame is determined by your official job description. But beyond that you have substantial freedom to choose the story you tell yourself. Often that story itself discourages you from becoming engaged.

"This Isn't What I Want to Spend My Life Doing"

One reason you may work halfheartedly is that you don't like your job. You may have hoped for another position. You may have grown tired of a job you once liked. You may be looking forward to a career change. You tell yourself that this isn't what you ought to be doing, and slacken your efforts. There is nothing wrong with deciding that a certain job is not your life's work. Too often, though, that decision is used as an excuse. Looking for another job might be a helpful step. Doing mediocre work in your current job is not.

"This Job Doesn't Use My Talents"

It is hard to stay interested in a job that is not challenging. Jobs can be boring, of course. If there is nothing to your job except simple repetitive tasks, you might even find it alienating. If a robot could do your job, you might suspect that you are considered no better than a robot.

If you accept a description of your job that includes no intellectual challenge, then it is no surprise that you turn away from it, like a teenager offered the chance to play with a toddler's toys. Yet it is rarely inevitable that you accept a limited range of responsibilities. Why not take on challenging work in addition to what you have been assigned? In the short run, doing only what you are told is easier. There is less work, and less chance of getting into trouble. In the long run, however, you'll find yourself staggering under the burden of a deadening job.

"Nothing I Do Matters"

That work should be challenging is not enough. If your work doesn't matter, you will be reluctant to put much energy into it. Someone writing a memo that will be filed away in a drawer and forgotten works with less diligence than one whose memo will be read at the next board meeting. If you see your job as one that makes no difference, you will have little chance of motivating yourself.

PRESCRIPTION: REFRAME YOUR JOB TO INCLUDE ENGAGING CHALLENGES

Whatever the reason for your disengagement, there is no point in waiting for someone else to motivate you. It is up to you. With practice you can develop the habit of becoming fully involved in what you are doing while you are doing it. The more skilled you are at becoming fully engaged — even if only briefly — the more productive and satisfied you will be. It is not a question of ordering yourself to feel committed. You cannot produce feelings on command. You *can* do things that in turn will affect your feelings.

Just as one frame — the way you think of your job — can hold you back, a different frame can energize you. Below are some components of a frame that you can adopt for yourself.

Make the Commitment Smaller

A young woman graduated from college having distinguished herself in creative writing. She had dreams of being a novelist.

To support herself she took a job writing advertising copy. One night she complained to her uncle that she had gotten a poor performance review. "But who cares? Persuading people to buy more laundry soap just isn't what I want to do with my life," she said.

"If that's the way you think about it," her uncle replied, "no wonder they don't like your work. Neither do you. You told me you plan to stay there for at least a few months. During that time you can learn to write words that deliver an impact. You can learn the difference between effective ads and ineffective ones — between powerful phrases and weak ones. You will enjoy your work more if you immerse yourself in it for several hours a day. While you are doing it, do the best damn job you can."

The young graduate did not need to convince herself that her current job was her life's work. But she did learn to convince herself to make it *today's* work. By changing the question she asked herself, she made the job more attractive.

Instead of asking yourself, "Is this my life's work?" ask yourself, "Would I be better off if I did something else for the next hour?" (If "yes," quit and do it.) If the answer is "no," then you have good reason to dive in and give it your best. You are not committing 100 percent of your time, nor is it for the rest of your life. Yet while you are doing something, you will enjoy it more and get more out of it if you put more into it.

The larger a commitment, the harder it is to commit. Fractionating a commitment makes it easier to swallow. Decide a day at a time, or an hour at a time, that the task in front of you is worth doing now.

Find Opportunities to Use Your Best Skills

It is frustrating to do work that does not require any creativity. Your job may require tasks that a robot could do just as well.

But unlike a robot, you can decide that you will do more than the job requires.

Roger's father, Walter Fisher, once told him about taking a job at a plumbing supply warehouse, years before he became a lawyer. Walter's job was to inspect barrels of cast-iron elbows and tees, sorting out the flawed ones. Bored, he began sorting the rejected parts according to the type of flaw that made them unacceptable. He noticed that most defects were at the bends. He hurried to get done early, and then went to look at the machine that made the parts, and suggested a change in the design of the casting molds.

Unfortunately, his boss calculated that the cost of improving the molds was greater than the cost of paying a boy to sort out the rejects. Walter then spent his spare time on another challenging task, that of finding a better job. He soon left the plumbing warehouse, but not before trying his best to turn a monotonous, low-skill job into one that gave him a challenge and offered benefit to his employer. A teenager who has been offered the chance to play only with a toddler's toys can take on the task of figuring out why some toys are more stimulating than others.

It isn't possible to make every job more fun and more productive — sometimes a ditch digger just has to dig a ditch. But even there . . .

Take time to contribute — even when it is not your job. One way to increase your energy at work is to help a colleague with a problem. You find a fresh challenge — and may see yourself having an impact. You can choose to take on a new task, and that task can lead you to be more engaged and more productive. One of the best ways to improve your own skills is to help others improve theirs. You can undertake to pass on some of your skills to a less experienced coworker. A steelworker in Texas came up with the idea of spending one evening a week with a coworker who was a new immigrant from mainland China. The Texan helped him improve his English, taught him the ins and outs of operating one of the plant machines, and heard fascinating accounts of life in a small Chinese town.

Expand your job to include things that aren't being done. Stuart worked in a teachers' clearinghouse to which instructors submitted materials they had prepared that were then made available to other faculty. For years the office had simply mailed out copies of materials in response to requests. Stuart thought a lot about how to make the clearinghouse more effective. Touching base with his superiors, he actively solicited materials and encouraged teachers to prepare new ones to meet needs. He produced and circulated catalogs, bought published books by local teachers at wholesale, and sold them at a fair discount. He put together sets of materials on special subjects, developed marketing strategies, and offered materials on the Internet. Stuart turned the clearinghouse from a subsidized operation into a significant revenue generator. He was soon appointed its director. He has now been hired away to do even more challenging work.

Every job has duties that need to be performed. Rarely, if ever, do job descriptions impose limits. Often the easiest way to make a job more challenging is to think of it as including things that you could do that would be good for the organization *and* good for you.

You may worry that taking on matters outside your formal jurisdiction might get you in trouble. There are risks in trespassing on someone else's turf. And yet there may be even greater risks in not lending a hand. A young woman in Boston who wanted to become a psychologist worked as a teacher in the children's unit of a psychiatric hospital. The children in her care often became unruly. The two psychologists assigned to the unit would stay in their offices, doing paperwork, while she tried to calm the children. The psychologists said that managing such crises was not part of their job. This went on until the hospital was taken over by a large medical services company that wanted to reduce staff. The new head of the hospital was walking through the children's unit and observed the teacher valiantly trying to contain a violent eruption, while the two psychologists continued to sit in their offices. He walked into the offices and informed them both that they were fired.

Imagine that you are a manager charged with laying off 20 percent of the workers in your department. You have to decide whom you will let go — the people who look for things that need doing, or those who do only what they are told. For the employees, which approach is in fact safer?

SECOND, CLARIFY A VISION OF JOINTLY USING THIS SKILL: EVERYONE BECOMES FULLY ENGAGED

Just as you sometimes slack off, you can see the same thing happening to others. It may be a few individuals who feel left out — or it may be a whole department or all the workers on a factory floor.

Before you can decide how to encourage involvement, you need to figure out why so many people are disengaged now.

PROBLEM: THE MORE PEOPLE WORKING TOGETHER, THE GREATER THE RISK OF DISENGAGEMENT

Alone, you face the problem of getting yourself committed to what you are doing. When a large group is working together, the situation is worse. Some of the reasons that people are not engaged are the same ones you experience when you work alone: the work is not challenging, or it seems not to matter how well it is done. Other reasons stem from the diminished urgency felt in a crowd.

Some Feel Left Out

The word "engagement" is used in two senses. It can simply mean participation in some activity. Or it can refer to an emotional state of commitment to a goal, a task, or an idea. The two meanings are closely related. Participating with others in an activity — whether fighting a war or painting a fence — tends to produce a feeling of commitment. Being left out of an activity, particularly an interesting or important one — produces alienation.

The most important activity for producing engagement is planning one's own work. One powerful cause of frustration is feeling that you have lost control. Carrying out another's detailed instructions rarely gives as much satisfaction as does exercising discretion. When people see no chance of doing more than follow orders, they feel less responsibility. "Let the boss worry about it." Withdrawal leads to poor performance, which tends to intensify dislike for what one is doing.

We Let Others Take Responsibility

One way in which working in a group is different from working alone is that we rely on others to do a given task — and they rely on us. The most commonly noted aspect of group behavior is a diminished sense of personal responsibility. The larger the group, the less responsibility each person feels. You mind your own garden and assume that someone will do anything else that needs to be done.

Medical studies show that you have a better chance of surviving a heart attack if only one other person is present than you do if many are nearby. In a crowd, each person expects someone else to help, maybe assuming that someone else is better qualified. When no one else does help, each person thinks that there is no problem. The same reaction happens in an organization. Everyone sits by and watches a group become disabled.

To avoid this problem, organizations assign different tasks to different people. Unfortunately, the way we assign tasks often creates as many problems as it solves.

We Divide Work Poorly

Often tasks are assigned almost at random. A manager realizes that he needs to follow up on some overdue receivables. As he worries about it, a subordinate comes into his office to discuss something else. It is not hard to guess who gets handed a new task.

Such assignments may not be truly haphazard. In fact, there is an implicit criterion operating here — "Give the job to whomever is nearby when the issue comes up." Once we articulate the implicit criterion, we can see that it is not likely to be the best for assigning tasks. We often apply equally poor criteria:

- Give another task to the one who works the hardest.
- Assign a job to the one who will complain least.
- Give a task to the one who is most pleasant to have around (or, if the task will be performed elsewhere, give it to the one who is least pleasant to have around).

These criteria harm the individual and the organization. They misallocate labor, since they have nothing to do with maximizing the group's output or matching tasks with skills or interests. They encourage uncooperative behavior — like complaining and resisting new assignments. Those who resist are allowed to take it easy in the short term. In the long run, they miss the chance to expand their skills and prove themselves.

Another common criterion, "Give each task to the person who is most skilled at it," sounds better than it is. Too much work may pile up on one person who is particularly skillful. In one academic department we know, the deputy director is such a person. He is a gifted writer and teacher. Few people in the world match his expertise in his subject. Yet he is often called away from using those talents because he is also the best person in the office to deal with the computers, balance the books, and negotiate with the university administration. Others could also do these tasks, if not as well. Because he is so good at the administrative work, he does less of the more important tasks of which he is capable. The fault lies in the poor job we often do of dividing tasks among people.

VISION: EVERYONE, OR ALMOST EVERYONE, IS FULLY ENGAGED

Ideally you would see everyone in the organization working up to her full potential. Each person would have a job she found important and interesting — and would use all her skills and energy to see that it is done well. While we may never reach the utopia of total engagement from everyone, it is still helpful to identify practices that tend to produce more commitment. What sort of procedures could we adopt that would foster such a situation?

Do Your Best to Offer Each Person an Attractive Role

It is easier to commit yourself to some jobs than to others. The challenge in organizing a group is to arrange roles to maximize the satisfaction that each person gets from a job.

We all have emotional interests in our jobs. People will be committed to the extent that a job serves their emotional interests. The first step is to take stock of what those interests are:

Respect.

How we are regarded by coworkers affects how we regard ourselves. If each of us sees our job as one that is worthy of respect, then we will be happier and work harder.

Autonomy.

If able to choose how we fulfill our responsibilities, we feel more ownership of the tasks, and more commitment to doing them well.

Impact.

We want to know that our efforts are producing a result. We get satisfaction in being able to see, touch, measure, or count the products of our labors.

Strive to serve those emotional interests. When someone keeps himself apart, it is often from the feeling that he has nothing to offer, or that the group doesn't need his contribution. His withdrawal, in turn, increases others' tendency to leave him out. One challenge for a leader (or a lateral leader), is to find something that this person can do well, and suggest a task for the group that needs that ability.

The military chief of staff of a West African country attended a negotiation course at Harvard Law School. He was exceptionally skillful at getting each of his fellow students to play an active part in class discussions. Impressed with his ability to foster participation, the teachers asked him how he did it. He told them, "If I have a soldier under me who does little work and is not liked by his comrades it is a problem. It slows everything down and hurts the company's morale. What I do is to find a special job for him. If he is a fast runner, I give him the next important message to take to another post. If he is a musician, I remind the troops they need to create a song for an upcoming national holiday. When the troops see that he is useful they become more friendly. Soon he is working as hard as anyone. In class I watch people to find topics that interest them. I notice when they sit up and pay attention. Then I ask the quiet one to say something about it."

An appointed leader is not the only person who can find a way to integrate an isolated teammate. In his country's army, the general had the power of command. He had no such authority in our classroom. Yet he was equally effective in encouraging lagging participants to contribute.

Almost everyone can do something useful. You don't need to create a boondoggle that wastes time and resources to make people feel important. It usually requires just a little thought to find something that needs doing that an "outsider" can do. In fact, it is easy to find a respected, interesting task that lets people contribute something useful. (Each chapter in this book contains a number of such ideas.)

Assume That Contributing Ideas Is Everyone's Job

You can invite everyone to take part in setting purposes, thinking, and learning from what you do together. If you have read the earlier chapters, this advice is not new. It does bear repeating. Having everyone take part in thinking improves the quality of the thinking. With a larger pool of ideas, there is a better chance that you will hit on a good one. In addition, it treats everyone with respect. It lets colleagues know that their thoughts are valued. They are likely to give their best if their work calls upon their abilities — especially their ability to think and make judgments.

People will be committed to goals that they help set. After helping formulate a goal, few will argue that it is unreasonable. Each is committed to a plan when he has helped to think it through. Team members are more likely to adopt a new way of doing things if each participated in the meeting where past performance was reviewed and changes formulated. One of the best features of this book's advice about setting purposes, thinking systematically, and learning from experience, is that it provides a framework for inviting everybody to offer ideas. And it does so without taking decision-making authority away from the appointed managers.

The coach of a British professional football (what Americans call soccer) club concluded that his players did not think enough about the game. They were slow to react to challenges posed by the opposition's style. The team's star player was one who needed most to widen his thinking. His main interest in life was to score as many goals as possible himself. He failed to focus on play making, passing, and supporting his teammates on defense. He cared more about improving his own statistics than about the success of the team.

The coach determined to get the star and other players more involved in preparing for games. The next afternoon he took them onto the training pitch, divided them up, gave each group a ball, and told them to devise their own training activity. The initial reaction was reluctance. The star player was unimpressed, yet started to work with three or four teammates. Some minutes later the coach looked over to where they were working. They were completely engaged in trying out a new drill. The "reluctant star" was contributing with great enthusiasm, calling out suggestions and encouraging his colleagues. In later games he proved more of a team player, without losing his ability to score goals himself.

Share Responsibility for Dividing Work

You can promote the attitude that each person should do all she can by having everyone take part in dividing the work. No one is left just minding her own niche. Everyone is part of a team that is working to get everything done.

Ask each person to contribute information. Each person knows best what skills she possesses. Each of us knows what sort of work would be most energizing. Assigning jobs is an informal negotiation in which each task presumptively goes to the one with the necessary skills, for whom the task is a challenge, and who makes the most persuasive commitment. Being present, colleagues are able to ask questions, share their ideas, and volunteer for what they would like to do.

List the tasks, and then assign them. To make sure that everything that needs doing is going to get done, every task needs someone responsible for it. That person need not have the authority or the resources to do the job alone, but it is now his duty to do what he can to see that it gets done.

A routine practice is to list our purposes — long-term goals and results we would like to achieve — and the tasks required to meet them. Then we make sure that everyone has a task and every task has someone responsible for it.

Frame the success of the whole project as everyone's responsibility. There are few words more ominous for the future of an organization than "That's not *my* job." One risk of a clear allocation of responsibilities is that people take it as a release of responsibility for any other job. An initial planning meeting will never spot every task that needs attention. New needs and problems will arise as you progress. It is important to make clear that everyone shares responsibility for meeting the aims of the organization. Task assignments are a floor on responsibility, not a ceiling.

Use Better Criteria for Deciding Who Does What

A risk of soliciting input about job assignments is that people may push for assignments that serve them but not the organization. What if everyone wants to be on the long-term planning staff and no one wants to take out the garbage? Or if everyone wants to woo new customers and no one wants to deal with complaints from existing customers?

A routine practice of asking for input need not dilute decision-making power. Workers are given a chance to suggest options, but ultimately those in authority retain the power to act in the organization's interest. They merely have a broader spectrum of ideas to consider.

Moreover, if people understand the criteria for making decisions, they will take them into account. When the Harvard Negotiation Project teaches negotiation seminars, it employs a cadre of law students as teaching assistants. They work in pairs. One challenge the course instructors have is how to match partners who will be productive together. The students initially want to work with a friend. The faculty offer criteria that serve the needs of the program — balance of experience, complementary working styles, some concern with diversity — and ask the students to nominate partners for themselves. Time after time the teaching assistants name choices that meet the organization's interests. The final decisions are as good as or better than those that the faculty would have made unaided. And each teaching assistant has the satisfaction of having freely chosen a partner, and the pleasure of being chosen. In the same way, allowing workers to suggest job assignments in the light of well-chosen criteria allows them to feel that they have chosen their own tasks. The result is greater commitment to the work in front of them.

Every organization will need different criteria for dividing work. The following guidelines offer a good starting point.

Assign work to the smallest group that will be sufficient. Resources are likely to be most efficiently used when each task is allocated to a lean group. The group should be small enough that members have to work hard.

Delegate work to the lowest level competent to do it. Day-to-day responsibility for carrying the ball — for example, keeping a particular customer happy — is too often kept at the level of the senior person who is ultimately responsible. It is generally a good idea to delegate a task down. Delegation does not mean that the recipient now has the discretion to make all decisions with respect to that job. Rather, the recipient now has the job of going forward until further guidance or authority is needed, and of seeking that guidance or authority. The amount of instruction to give when delegating is a function of the recipient's competence. If the person knows enough about the task to complete it, he does not need detailed instructions. Explain the desired result, and leave the rest up to the subordinate.

Assign each person the most important task of which she is capable. Giving each task to the person most skilled at it may dump too many tasks at the door of a someone who could be doing more challenging things. A better approach is to maximize the contribution each person makes by assigning each one the most important job that he or she can handle.

It is not always possible to implement all these guidelines. For example, you may need only one person to negotiate a deal when there are three people for whom that is the most important task they could do. But when it is possible to follow them, they tend to produce better results.

THEN LEAD:
FOSTER A CLIMATE THAT INVITES
ENGAGEMENT

ONE TASK YOU CAN TAKE ON IS IMPROVING THE COLLABORATION

The authors suggest offering each person a job that she finds challenging, exciting, and worthy of respect. Here is one for you, the reader: take on the job of improving the way the people in your organization collaborate. Bored? This task will be fresh and exciting. Fear that your work does not matter? If you can promote better habits of group interaction you could be the most important person in the company. One place you can start is to promote habits that will lead to more energetic and committed performance from your colleagues.

Offer a Diagnosis: Current Roles Limit Responsibility

Consider once again the case of the apathetic soccer team. What if the coach had not been effective at stimulating engagement? If you are a minor player with no particular influence — say, a second-string fullback — is there anything you could do? One approach is to go to the coach and offer your thoughts — a diagnosis — on why the team may be performing halfheartedly.

YOU: Have you got a minute? I wanted to run a thought past you. You said to us after our last game that the lads don't think enough about strategy on the field.

COACH: And you do? Looking for a spot on the starting eleven, are we?

YOU: Well, yes, but not at this moment. I was trying to figure out *why* we don't think very hard out on the field. Seems to me that before and after every game you do the thinking for us. You review the game films and tell us what you see, you design the practice exercises. We don't have to think about anything. By the time we run out on the field we're in the habit of leaving it to you.

COACH: Perhaps there's something to that.

YOU: Can you think of other explanations? There might be something else.

With luck the coach will start to think about ways to remedy the diagnosis without further help from you. If he doesn't, you may lead him to take the next step.

Ask for Direction: "How Shall We Get Them to Take on More?"

If you go to the coach and tell him the best course to pursue, he might easily think that you are stepping out of line. If he then focuses on putting you back in your place, you will lose the chance to improve the team's methods. Instead of telling the coach what to do, present yourself as a loyal subordinate asking up the chain of command for instructions.

YOU: I know you've been telling us to do more thinking on the field. I suppose you'll start with ways to get us thinking *off* the field. What are some things we could do that would get our brains in better shape?

COACH: I suppose I could give you each a tape of the game video to watch before the review. Do you think the lads will really apply themselves to it?

YOU: I would. I think everyone would if you told them why it was a good idea. Is there anything else we could do?

COACH: Hmm. After practice we might have them talk over their impressions of the game before I tell them my views.

YOU: If we have the chance to say something I won't try to skip postgame meetings anymore. Great! I won't take up any more of your time.

COACH: That's okay.

If you ask first, and the coach doesn't have a direction, then you can offer your own. If he does have an idea, and you don't like it, you can offer another idea. Leave the decision up to him. You trot off to practice and let him decide.

DO SOMETHING: CONSULT BEFORE DECIDING

Some years ago a British oil tanker broke down in the Persian Gulf without the needed spare part — which the captain should have had on board. To radio London and have the part flown out would be expensive, slow, and especially embarrassing. In desperation, he called together a number of subordinates and put the situation to them. The radio operator, from whom the captain expected nothing, told the group that a crew member had just received a message from his brother who was on the company's sister ship. Due to an unexpected change of plans it was in the area. The captain promptly radioed his fellow captain, who confirmed that he had the needed spare part on board, and they arranged a rendezvous.

Inviting others to give you advice will make them feel appreciated and respected, which in turn will lead them to work effectively. Of course, another reason to ask for advice is to get useful advice.

Find Something Useful in Their Contribution

We all know how easy it is to dismiss someone else's suggestion. And that is one sure way of getting others to switch off and stop contributing. Instead, start from the assumption that they thought their idea was useful. If you don't see how, ask them to explain.

It is worth your time. When Roger's wife, Caroline, had promised that he would attend a dinner party that he had no interest in, he repeated one of his favorite slogans, "ACBD — Always Consult Before Deciding." After a moment she replied, "That means 'NGAD — Never Get Anything Done.'" Involving others does take time. And there are occasions when you do not have the time. If there is a fire in the kitchen, don't call the family together to ask for ideas. But most situations are not like that. Time spent involving others often means that better action will be taken with more commitment and more success. In the end you are more likely to save time.

Asking for advice makes you look more competent. You may be reluctant to ask others for advice because you fear it reflects badly on you. A manager may be reluctant to ask subordinates for fear that she will lose their confidence. There is a certain romanticism about rugged individualism. The hero of a movie is often a loner. By seeking help we may be abandoning this hero's role.

But if you think about times when someone asked you for advice, you probably did not lose respect for them. Quite the contrary. Shortly after Edward M. Kennedy was first elected to the U.S. Senate, he asked the defeated candidate to give him the names of his "brain trust" of academic advisers. Finding himself grounded in Boston during a February snowstorm, Kennedy phoned one of these professors and asked if he could come around for an hour to pick his brain. Arriving at Harvard, the senator realized that he did not even know in what field the professor was supposed to be an expert. Undeterred, the senator asked his first question: "What would be some good questions for me to ask?" The senator did not lower his status with the professor. (Roger was left with the feeling that Kennedy was pretty smart.) Most people are like that. We are reluctant to be seen as needing help, but we like to be seen to help.

Don't let them take over. You may hesitate to involve others because you fear that they will expect their views to be automatically adopted. If you ask your mother for her thoughts on

planning your wedding she may tell you exactly what to do —
and be upset if you don't follow her advice to the letter. If you
ask a colleague for advice you may walk into a similar situation. A request for advice can easily be misheard as a delegation of authority. It helps to make clear the kind of response
you are seeking.

There's a lot you don't know. We never know how much we
don't know. The tanker captain could not have known what
the radio operator knew. We all make assumptions about the
contributions that others can make. And we are often mistaken.

The chairman of a Canadian conglomerate who had been
promoted rapidly within the company noted that one of his
big lessons had been to learn that he was not chairman
because he knew answers but because he knew how to find
them, and had the judgment to separate good answers from
bad ones. As he went up the ladder, he said, his job had
changed from telling subordinates to asking them.

Consulting before deciding, like other methods of increasing
involvement, serves two purposes. It lets us draw on a wider
base of ideas and talent. And it tends to increase engagement
and commitment from those consulted for their thoughts.

7 FEEDBACK

EXPRESS APPRECIATION, OFFER ADVICE

What we are able to achieve depends on how well we use the resources available to us. When we work with others we have a tremendous opportunity to help one another improve our skills and thus increase those resources. We can observe one another's performance far better than we can judge our own. A baseball player can't see himself bat — especially when he is trying to concentrate on the pitcher — so he needs a teammate to check his swing for any problems. Moreover, everyone brings different skills and experiences to our joint work. We all know good pointers that the others don't yet know.

Increasing the effectiveness of the feedback you offer one another can make a tremendous impact on your productivity and efficacy. And you can encourage others to give (and receive) feedback better by doing a better job yourself, by envisioning better practices and attitudes among your colleagues, and by helping make that vision take shape.

FIRST, DEVELOP A PERSONAL SKILL: LEARN HOW TO OFFER SUPPORTIVE FEEDBACK

PROBLEM: WE FAIL TO HELP OUR COLLEAGUES WHEN WE COULD

Considering the benefits of exchanging feedback, we ought to do it all the time. Yet we know that is not the case. When law students return to school after a summer at a big firm, their usual complaint is that they got little guidance or feedback on their work. One hears the same stories from junior consultants, investment bankers, sales reps, managers. And senior people in organizations often complain that their subordinates don't notice or appreciate their hard work.

We all probably recognize why this happens — we ourselves rarely take the time to help someone do better. We watch a colleague or boss, and think, "He's making a big mistake." But we don't meddle. We don't point out mistakes (or effective practices, either). We think of saying something. We may even put it on our list of things to do. But it stays there day after day. There is always something we'd rather be doing. The result is that others are not learning much or getting much support from us. How come?

DIAGNOSIS: WE AVOID GIVING FEEDBACK BECAUSE WE LACK THE SKILL TO DO IT WELL

You probably don't avoid helping your colleagues out of laziness. It is more likely that you have tried and got burned. Perhaps the recipient got angry. He may have reacted by pointing out your failings. So now you maintain a détente — with neither of you raising a subject that would cause the other anxiety.

When you try to improve your skill in offering feedback, your first problem is that you are unclear about your goal.

Assume that you have watched a colleague, an assistant, or your boss working. You consider talking about it. For what purpose? Is it to increase his morale? To point out some error? To score a point? To reward good behavior? To make a progress report?

The most common impulse is to criticize. You know from experience that this is not well received. So you try to offer "constructive criticism." But the distinction between "constructive" and "destructive" misses the point. It is the assumption that your purpose is "criticism" that needs questioning. "Critic" suggests someone who judges movies or restaurants — someone who is there to give a thumbs-up or thumbs-down, and move on to their next subject. A critic helps others decide whether to go to a movie or reject it. You will not be moving on. You will continue to work with your assistant, your colleague, your boss. You cannot easily choose to avoid working with them. Rather, you want to improve the way they do things.

PRESCRIPTION: SEPARATE APPRECIATION FROM ADVICE FROM EVALUATION

You want to give feedback that will help you and your coworkers get more done. There are at least three distinct strategies for doing that. Depending on the purpose you have in mind, you should give feedback differently:

To encourage the recipients and improve their morale.

Your purpose here is to affect your colleagues' feelings about work — to make it more likely that they will work hard. You want them to feel confident about tackling a hard task. You want them to feel enthusiastic about coming to work every day. You want them to feel gratified that others notice their work. They will then work harder, be more likely to stay with the organization, and probably do a better job.

To help them improve their skills.

Your purpose in this case is to help your colleagues perform more skillfully. You want them to learn from experience — theirs and yours — and do a better job next time. You cannot force your colleagues to do these things. They control their own behavior. Your purpose is to provide them with ideas and suggestions that they can choose to adopt.

To make personnel decisions.

The organization may need a guide in making future choices about who will be promoted, who deserves a bonus, who needs more training, and who will be let go. One of your purposes may be to develop data that will help the organization make these decisions wisely. You will want to communicate your evaluation to the recipients, so that they know how they are doing in the organization, and have the chance to change their behavior.

You will need different methods to achieve such distinct purposes. Thus, there are at least three different kinds of feedback that may be appropriate in a given situation:

- APPRECIATION is expression of gratitude or approval of another's effort. It is an expression of emotion, designed to meet an emotional need.
- ADVICE (or COACHING) consists of suggestions about particular behavior that should be repeated or changed. It focuses on the performance, rather than judging the person.
- EVALUATION is ranking the subject's performance in relation to that of others or against an explicit or implicit set of standards.

Often we don't think clearly about our purposes in giving feedback, and consequently we confuse the kind of feedback we are offering. If you lack a single clear purpose your feedback may do more harm than good. A social worker, before giving an important talk to a professional gathering on testing homeless children for emotional disturbance, tries out her talk on a few colleagues. They think her talk is pretty good, but can tell that she is nervous. To build up her confidence, they tell her, "It's wonderful — absolutely perfect." One useful purpose is to build up her confidence. Another is to help make a good presentation even better. Her friends implied that there were no improvements to be made — and the social worker lost an opportunity to refine her talk.

A better approach would be to say, "I enjoyed your talk. My guess is that your audience will like it as well." That could be followed by saying, "If you like, we could spend some time trying to make it even better."

The habit you want to develop is to know your purpose when you offer feedback, and to make your comments in a form appropriate to accomplishing that purpose.

Separate the Different Kinds of Feedback

Trying to accomplish two or more of these purposes at once is difficult. Most of us have a limited supply of attention, especially when confronted with a touchy subject like an assessment of our performance. A college professor spends a large part of her weekend writing exhaustive comments on a student's paper. When it is handed back, the student flips to the last page to see the grade. If he gets an A, he is overjoyed. If he gets a C he mopes the rest of the day, muttering that the grade was unfair. In either case he spends little time trying to learn from all the suggestions the professor had made. The emotional impact of being graded tends to drown out advice on improving performance.

It is best to offer different kinds of feedback at different times. At the very least, you should explicitly signal when you move from one purpose to another. Above all, it helps to separate both advice and appreciation from the anxiety that typically accompanies a performance review — evaluation. Most times, evaluation is the one that is least likely to be helpful, and most likely to distract from your other two purposes.

Check Your Purpose with the Recipient

A man leaves work early to make a special dinner for his wife. After eating the elaborate meal, her first words are "I think this sauce could use more pepper." She will be lucky if he doesn't throw the sauce at her. She is answering the question, "How could he improve?" while he is listening for "Does she appreciate me for all the trouble I went to?" He is left to wonder about or speculate on her purpose. Would she have preferred to have eaten out? Is she upset about something else? Is she trying to hurt his feelings?

It makes good sense to discuss the sort of feedback you want to share, and check whether your counterpart is interested in hearing it. "I'd like to offer you some suggestions about what I have seen of your work, and see whether they make sense to you. Would that be useful?" Asking permission allows them to prepare, so they will not be surprised. And it makes the coaching session something they have chosen to take part in, rather than an involuntary trip to the woodshed.

SPECIFIC PRACTICES: A FEW TECHNIQUES THAT WILL HELP YOU PROVIDE USEFUL FEEDBACK

In light of these general prescriptions for improving your skill in offering and seeking feedback, there are a number of specific ideas and suggestions.

Express Appreciation to Motivate

When working within a group, we all sometimes feel anxious for fear that we are being rejected or excluded. Appreciation is designed to counter such concerns and to raise morale by indicating that one "belongs," one matters — one's effort and contribution are appreciated. Therefore you want to direct your appreciation to the individual as a human being. His feelings will be affected more by directing comments toward him personally, rather than toward his actions. "I am impressed by *you*." "I enjoy working with *you*." "*You* are an asset to this team." "I think *you're* the cat's pajamas."

Appreciate early and often. When should you offer appreciation? Always. It's always a good time to spend a moment boosting someone else's mood, and thus boosting their productivity. The cost is low: it takes only a minute to drop by someone's office and say, "I'm grateful for your hard work." The benefit is high: a chance to improve their productivity, make them easier to get along with, and make it easier for them to accept advice or coaching at another time.

You can affect others' feelings by revealing your own. The goal of appreciation is to alter another's feelings about work. The quickest and surest route to their feelings is through your own.

The need for appreciation is an emotional need. You are afraid of what others might be thinking about you. This is as true for the most accomplished person in the company as it is for the newest recruit. Sometimes even very distinguished people fear that no one respects them. It is a subjective fear about other people's subjective opinions. Thus the most direct way to give appreciation is to allow the other person to see into your subjective feelings about her.

- "I was happy with your work."
- "I am proud to be your colleague."
- "I feel confident leaving the office when I know that you are here to handle any problems."
- "I am impressed with how hard you try."
- "I know what it is like to have to work all night."

Mentioning your feelings makes it clear that having emotional needs does not make people weak or contemptible — it recognizes that the people who work in professional organizations are still people.

Letting them see into your feelings can be risky. They are likely to spot insincerity. That makes it crucial that you first get your own thoughts sorted out — that you negotiate with yourself to empathize sincerely with the subjects, and look carefully at all that they contribute.

Find something to appreciate. You might object: "How can I offer appreciation if I am not happy with their performance? Wouldn't that be dishonest?"

It is easiest to express appreciation when the result is spectacular. But what about when the results are lousy? Sometimes poor results are caused by something wholly beyond the person's control. The pastry chef was in no way responsible for the power failure that occurred just after he put the soufflé in the oven. Nonetheless, the result was a total disaster. Whatever the result, you should commend him for his effort and commiserate with how it must feel to have all that effort wasted.

Recently the family of a victim who had drowned in high surf off Martha's Vineyard asked the local newspaper to help them locate the passerby who had plunged into the surf risking his own life in a vain attempt to rescue the drowning man. The family quite wisely — despite their grief — wanted to thank the would-be rescuer personally and express their appreciation for his efforts. A performance may be brave and skillful without producing good results.

Or a performance may be bungled because of lack of skill, lack of experience, or lack of physical strength. Still, one may deserve an "A for effort." Effort deserves an honest expression of appreciation whatever the results. And even if the effort was halfhearted, you should distinguish effort, performance, and results from the worth of the person involved.

A while back a rainstorm hit. The husband had furled the big beach umbrella in the center of the outdoor glass-topped table. His wife suggested that perhaps he should bring the umbrella indoors to avoid the risk that wind would blow over the table and smash the glass. The husband decided it was not worth going out in the rain. After all, the table had blown over before without harm. By morning the glass tabletop had been smashed into a thousand pieces all over the lawn where the children regularly ran barefoot.

Here the effort was poor and the results awful. Yet rather than tell him how to do better next time, the wife wisely gave him a hug, recognizing that he was more in need of understanding and support now than if he had done a better job.

When somebody knows that his performance should have been better, it is wise to avoid rubbing his nose in it. One can empathize with those responsible for a failure: "Boy. I know just how you feel. I have done the same. I chalk it up to education."

Dishonest praise is a mistake. Finding something worth acknowledging, even if it seems like looking for a needle in a haystack, is usually worthwhile. And if found, it is worth appreciating honestly. Getting some emotional reward will give others the courage to keep trying. If they are going to keep trying to please you, they have to know that pleasing you is possible.

Offer Advice to Improve Performance

The purpose of giving advice or coaching is to help others improve their skills or develop their potential. Direct the coaching toward what they do and how they do it. The purpose is not to show that you are smarter than the recipient. It is not to negotiate for something you want. "I think you should take out the garbage (so I don't have to)," does not constitute coaching. "If you are trying to take out the garbage, here's an idea that might help," does. Coaching is most effective when it meets an interest of the recipient — the interest in getting better at what he or she is doing.

Appreciation is directed toward the person: "Thank *you* for helping." For coaching, the opposite is true. It is most effective when it is aimed at the *performance* — at particular behavior that the recipient can choose to do or not do — and away from the person. It focuses on choosing between different methods of getting something done.

There will be less emotional resistance if the conversation is depersonalized. You are more likely to get better work if you focus on how to improve the work rather than on how to improve the human being. The model is two colleagues discussing different techniques for achieving a goal — like two anglers pondering which lure would catch the most fish. The comparison is between the way the recipient is working now, and some possible alternatives.

Make it a conversation. The best coaching is not a lecture. When you are offering your observations try to remember that you are just one observer, with all your failings and biases. You are not endowed with perfect insight, knowledge, or skill.

Start by asking questions. You need to seek information as well as to offer your own views. If you are going to offer advice about how to perform a task, you need to be clear what the recipient was trying to do. Once a young army officer was acting as adjutant to a general. The two were reviewing a meeting that had just concluded, and the young officer advised his boss at length on how he could have helped a consultant who was part of their task force be a more productive participant in such a large meeting. The general interrupted him. "I didn't *want* him to do a better job at that meeting. I wanted to see him go on and on like an idiot so that everyone there would know why I had to fire him," explained the general. This shift in purpose certainly shifted the advice the young officer might offer. To give good advice, you need to understand what the recipient of the advice is trying to accomplish.

The best advice on when to give advice usually comes from the recipient. You can tell him that you would like to offer some suggestions, and ask when would be a good time. He will then feel that he has chosen to receive coaching, and will likely be more open to it. And you will get the chance to offer advice when it is most likely to be helpful. Unfortunately, with some people there is never a good time. You may want to insist that such a person at least listen and consider your suggestions.

You will do a better job coaching if you give the recipient a chance to direct you. There may be a particular aspect of her performance on which your colleague would like your thoughts. She is more likely to listen attentively and try to change her behavior if she has decided that she should improve in that area. A coach may also inquire into the recipient's personal preferences. One lecturer at a law school regularly invites suggestions from any student or visiting colleague — *and* asks that all observations and advice be reserved until classes are over for the week, so that the advice will not distract him from his immediate performance.

It is often useful to ask a recipient what he thinks of his performance, and how it could be improved. "I have some suggestions. Before I offer my ideas I'd like to hear your thoughts about how you might do better." If he comes up with the same suggestion that you were planning to offer, all the better. It is more likely to affect his behavior if he views it as his own idea with which you concur.

Even when you are trying to advise or coach someone, you are trying to help the recipient change his own behavior, not change it for him. Ultimately others will decide what their behavior will be. Even subordinates cannot be watched all day. Your attempt to change their behavior will succeed only if you leave it to them to decide to change their approach.

Reinforce what WORKED WELL. Rather than thinking of observations as divided between positive and negative, they are more usefully divided into two categories: what Worked Well (WW) and what to Do Differently (DD). Thus, instead of *evaluating* the performance ("That was great" or "That could use some work,") you can reinforce its strengths and develop concrete ways to improve it.

When you comment to others on their performance, there is a danger that you will focus on things that you didn't like and that you would like to see changed. As they say, "The nail that sticks up gets pounded down." You rarely notice those nails that were hammered in correctly in the first place. You forget to notice successes and to comment on them.

People can learn just as much from successes as from difficulties. Effective people are frequently unable to articulate what it is that they are doing well. Pointing out specific things that helped a performance makes it easier for an actor to repeat those things. It also helps him to formulate general principles that can be applied to other situations.

Where possible, try to frame your suggestions as positive reinforcement. "Do more of X," not "Do less of Y." Both have the same substantive meaning, but the first is less threatening. It is also more effective. If you have your head full of what you should not do, but don't know what you should do instead, it is not surprising if you keep doing what you shouldn't. As we all know, telling someone not to think of elephants doesn't work.

Relying on extending successes rather than rooting out mistakes has several benefits. The recipient knows that he is able to make the change suggested — because he has already done it in another case. He feels more confident because he was able to get it right at least part of the time. Finally, he knows that you saw the good part of his work, and is less likely to worry about your opinion of him.

Offer suggestions of what to DO DIFFERENTLY. It is not always possible to rely on positive reinforcement alone. You have to address aspects of another's performance that he needs to change. Often you tell the recipient what you don't like about his performance, and leave it up to him to come up with something better. Criticism without operational suggestions may do more harm than good. This is especially so if there is no time to work out how to do better.

Some years ago Alan was watching a leading English soccer team play a team from a much lower division. The ball was played across in front of the former's goal and was scrambled away by the other side for a corner. The captain clearly considered that his goalkeeper, an experienced international player, should have advanced and claimed the ball himself, thus clearing any danger. Accordingly, as their opponents prepared to take the corner, the captain proceeded to berate the goalkeeper angrily and at some length for the perceived error. When the corner was taken, the goalkeeper, presumably with the criticism still ringing in his ears, advanced much farther from his goal than usual to try to reach the ball. He failed — and the opposition scored what turned out to be the winning goal. To an onlooker it seemed highly improbable that he would have gone for the ball and that the goal would have been scored but for his captain's criticism. The captain's action might have relieved his own annoyance, but it did not help the goalkeeper use his skill.

A specific suggestion, made when the recipient has time to think, is more likely to lead to the desired change in behavior. You might tell someone, "It seems to me that you were pretty dumb to have the map and directions printed up in final form before asking anyone to try them out." Such a comment tends to engender resistance, defensiveness, and even counter-criticism. Specific suggestions are more helpful: "I have found that no matter how clearly I think that I have written out directions, it helps to have someone else try to follow them. Time and again I find that my directions contained unexpected ambiguities. So if time permits, I try not to duplicate directions without having them tested first. And I try to allow enough time for that to happen." "Here's how I think you might improve" is more useful than "You got this part wrong."

Don't offer too many suggestions in one sitting. Overload can happen when a subordinate leaves a performance review with a list of twenty things that he should change. He is likely to forget many of them before getting a chance to put them into practice. Worse, a great mass of changes looks intimidating and discouraging. When giving feedback orally, it is usually wise to confine yourself to two or three suggestions at the most. Let the recipient put them into practice before piling more on.

This chapter, for example, contains far too many illustrative suggestions for you, the reader, to be expected to absorb in one reading. Our advice to a reader: don't try to do everything at once. You can focus on just one bit of advice at a time, then come back to the book and pick out another suggestion to try. When giving oral feedback we don't have the luxury of storing it on a shelf and coming back to it from time to time. Keep it simple.

Share specific data and reasoning. We often offer advice that is too general to be useful. Jeff and Allen work in the sales department of a mobile phone manufacturer. They have just gotten back from a meeting with a potential distributor.

JEFF: How do you think that went? Any tips for me?

ALLEN: It was great. Good job. Keep up the good work. Except for one thing: you have to be tough with these guys. Don't make them think that they can get a better deal than all the other distributors. We're just throwing away money when you do that.

JEFF: Yeah, but this is a really big deal for us, I had to make sure . . .

ALLEN: Exactly! That's why we have to make sure we protect our margin. Its a lot more important with a big distributor than with one of the small fry.

JEFF: Okay. I'll keep that in mind.

The more general the coaching advice, the more it is taken as a personal indictment, rather than a professional analysis of the behavior. It's not surprising that Jeff focuses on defending himself rather than trying to learn from Allen's comments. Since the idea is to see the good behavior again, it helps to be as specific as possible. Telling someone "good job" doesn't help him know which particular things to repeat. Specificity allows others to understand what exactly you saw them do, and why you liked it. That makes it more likely that they will make it part of their own thinking. Specificity also allows them to add other data that you may have missed, or explain their reasoning, in a way that might change your analysis. Remember, the goal is to find better methods, not to be right. Sharing the specific data makes us partners in the job of finding better methods.

Another version of the same scene might go something like this:

JEFF: How do you think that went? Any tips for me?

ALLEN: Well, I was really impressed with the way you set a relaxed, comfortable tone. For example, when the distributor asked why our products are more expensive than the competition's you had a couple of reasons ready, and you gave examples in your explanation. I thought it showed you were open to talking about tough issues, and encouraged her to be open with you about her concerns.

JEFF: Thanks. It's good working with you.

ALLEN: I also have a suggestion, if you would care to hear it.

JEFF: Sure, that would be fine.

ALLEN: Remember when you were explaining the policy about price protection? When we drop the price and the distributor has stock in the warehouse that she bought under the old price?

JEFF: Yeah.

ALLEN: I took note of what you said about it. You said, "We don't *usually* like to offer more than thirty days of price protection," and your tone struck me as rather tentative. I think that's why she pressed us for the ninety-day period. What led you to say it that way?

JEFF: C'mon, this is a really big deal. I didn't want the competition to get this distributor just because of the price protection. I wasn't going to gamble on losing her.

ALLEN: You're right, we would rather give on the price protection than lose the client. I think we might have gotten the thirty days and kept her. My recommendation would have been to present the deal we would like her to take in the best possible light, with a confident tone, and if she asks for more we talk about it. For instance, you might say, "We offer a thirty-day period to all of our distributors, and we don't know of anyone in the industry who offers more. Some manufacturers offer only fifteen days." Then, if she wants more, we can try to figure out why and find some way to accommodate her needs.

JEFF: Okay, what if she says that she heard that we sometimes make exceptions?

ALLEN: Well, one thing you can do is . . .

Being specific does take more time and effort. It also requires attention to the specific language used at the time. At the same time, it is an investment that is more likely to help someone actually learn a particular skill, perhaps saving time otherwise spent fixing their mistakes or doing further coaching.

Evaluate Only When Needed to Make a Personnel Decision

Frequently a manager has to decide who will be promoted, who will be put on probation, or who will be "downsized." And often such a manager will want to solicit the opinions of fellow employees whose judgment is based on closer observation than the manager's. Comparative evaluation against a scale or against the performance of others is rarely the best way to improve someone's performance. A broad conclusion that someone is the worst in the group is almost bound to discourage them, and convey no idea of what to do about it. Telling them that they are number one may cause them to relax and fails to communicate precisely what it is about their performance that they should replicate and build on.

One common mistake is to treat all feedback as evaluation. Evaluation is sometimes needed to give somebody "a kick in the pants" — to make them try harder. In selecting which of a dozen law students in an advanced negotiation seminar should be invited to become teaching assistants, Roger once asked all twelve to rank anonymously everyone in the class for their ability to be a good teaching assistant. No opportunity was given for collusion or bargaining. Eleven of the students ranked one student as number twelve, and one ranked that student as number one. The results suggested that that student needed some candid evaluation of how he was doing.

SECOND, CLARIFY A VISION OF JOINTLY USING THIS SKILL: AN ATMOSPHERE OF MUTUAL SUPPORT AND COACHING

By using practices like those described above you can develop your own skill in offering and seeking help in developing your abilities and those of your colleagues. What we want to achieve in an organization is the sort of atmosphere where it is customary to help each other learn and develop. Yet those of us who have worked in a business of any size are likely to be familiar with a different climate. Probably we are more familiar with situations where it is usual for us or others to do nothing at all — until it is too late.

The larger the number of people working together, the more difficult it is to establish open and easy feedback up, down, and across the organization. We don't know one another as well. The organization is likely to be more bureaucratic, and it is more difficult to know what is going on.

Paul's first regular job was in the claims department of an insurance company in Hartford. He did not immediately impress the more senior people in the department. He did not make major mistakes, but he had no great successes, either. The senior officers spent their time and effort with other workers. Paul's contemporaries had someone looking over their shoulders, marking up their reports, telling them where they should do things differently in order to improve. Since no one asked more of him, Paul assumed he was at the top of the class. When there was a cutback, Paul was astonished to learn that he was fired.

People in big organizations often complain that their work is ignored or unappreciated. Junior people want more attention from their superiors. Investment analysts, associates in a law firm, and young carpenters starting to learn their trade all complain that their work goes unnoticed and unguided.

Higher-ups within the same organizations have the same problem. Yet others are reluctant to give them advice, and especially loathe to point out any mistakes. Senior people find that their status inhibits them from getting the feedback they need. And they often feel that their experience, and their years of hard work, are unappreciated. No one pats them on the back for good work. They are supposed to encourage and motivate their subordinates, but who encourages *them*?

The problem is serious. Workers and professionals who find that their labors go unnoticed feel dissatisfied. They will likely reduce the amount of effort they put in. If no one notices how hard you are working, why bother? You can be equally ignored with less effort. Worse, it stifles improvement in performance. A factory can improve productivity by investing in plant and equipment. It can also, with some effort, improve the productivity of human beings.

Why is it that so often people in large organizations seem to "die on the vine"? Why are people who have been recruited for their ability and potential fired some time later for not fulfilling that potential?

DIAGNOSIS: UNFOUNDED ASSUMPTIONS
DISCOURAGE US FROM HELPING

The same reasons that you are not skilled in giving and inviting feedback apply to others as well. They do not understand the different purposes of giving feedback, nor do they know how to pursue each purpose. With a widespread lack of feedback skills, a culture tends to develop in which there is a set of unwritten assumptions that justify the lack of mutual support and coaching. Many of these assumptions discourage us from using our observations to help each other. The following are some common assumptions.

"We're Not Here to Flatter Each Other"

In 1949 William was a young finance officer at the Paris headquarters of the Marshall Plan. He had been working hard to prepare for an expected currency crisis in Austria. When the crisis occurred, Ambassador Averill Harriman flew to Vienna, leaving William in Paris. Harriman worked for a week in Austria while all banks were closed, and mediated a remarkable solution.

William told his colleague Roger that he intended to resign. "What am I doing here? Harriman doesn't need me. He did everything right without studying the problem for six months the way I did, and without even talking with me." Later Roger was surprised when Harriman mentioned, "Our young finance officer is a genius. When the crisis came that Saturday night, we could not find him. I had the security guards open his safe. William had foreseen the crisis and written a long draft memo on it. We made a copy of his draft. It was my bible all week. I just followed his advice." When Roger suggested that Harriman should tell the finance officer about the value of his work, the ambassador replied, "We didn't come over to Europe to sit around flattering each other. He was doing his job." Roger had to use all his powers of persuasion to get

Harriman to schedule an appointment to compliment the finance officer for a job well done.

We often fail to express appreciation because we don't realize how much most people benefit from being reassured and encouraged. Even more damaging are assumptions about what it means when someone offers appreciation to another.

"Anyone Who Needs Praise Is Weak"

Competent professionals get their satisfaction from doing good work. A real professional doesn't care what anyone else thinks, or so the notion goes. Many people feel embarrassed when their work is praised — because of the image that a truly strong person does not need to hear it. It is only the young, or the slow, who need to be "babied" or "have their hand held."

Unfortunately, these views ignore the fact that even the most competent expert is also a human being, with emotional needs and insecurities.

"Competent People Do Not Need to Be Told How to Do Their Jobs"

We all want to project an image of competence — to let others see our abilities in a favorable light. Unfortunately, we may act as though we need to maintain an illusion of perfection. We think that smart, talented professionals should not make mistakes. Just as you want to hide your mistakes so that others won't see them, you want to turn away advice, lest anyone see you as someone who needs it. We have all seen someone snap, "I already knew that!" to defend himself against the implication that he could profit from a friendly pointer.

We also try to cover up the fact that we are avoiding advice. We can't say, "Thanks, but I would rather not take advice. An illusion of perfection is more important to me than learning from a mistake." So instead we use indirect tactics to discourage colleagues from offering advice. We may deny that a mistake was made. We may express outrage at the presumption of the person who wants to help us. The perverse consequence of trying to maintain an image of flawless competence is that we avoid examining real mistakes and consider options for improving. Eventually, by trying to prove ourselves competent, we ensure we remain incompetent at many things, and particularly at learning.

"Coaching Is Something a Superior Does to a Subordinate"

If you admit that you do have something to learn about your job, you may be very particular from whom you will take advice. We assume that we listen to advice because the giver is smarter or more experienced. As a consequence, you will take advice from your boss, but a subordinate who tries to offer a suggestion is in for trouble. We rarely stop to think that the skills that get one promoted may not be the same as the expertise to coach a subordinate on every task. We lose the chance to get help from a junior colleague who has recently overcome the problem that we are facing.

This assumption about taking advice only from superiors is paired with another: that advice or coaching is the same as an order. If the recipient of coaching is supposed to follow the advice whether she agrees or not, then it can only flow downhill.

PRESCRIPTION: AN ORGANIZATION ADOPTS A BETTER SET OF ASSUMPTIONS

The vision you would like to create is of a group of people working together and operating on a more helpful set of working assumptions.

"Appreciation Makes Everyone Perform Better"

A Cambridge publisher was becoming increasingly depressed. His morale fell and so did the energy devoted to his work.

Every letter he read was just one more unhappy person with a complaint or a problem he had to deal with. As he coped with one grievance after another, he finally complained to his assistant that nobody seemed to appreciate anything he did. His assistant replied, "Oh no. Most of your mail is highly complimentary. People are always writing to thank you or congratulate you for something you did. Knowing how busy you are, I acknowledge those letters and put them in the file. I just give you the negative letters because they need your attention." The filtering system was quickly changed. When expressions of appreciation were allowed to come through, the publisher's morale and energy level both went up.

Subordinates, in particular, fail to realize how much difference they can make to a superior by expressing appreciation for what he or she has done. The truth is that people often work hard — and rise to the top — because they have a strong need to be appreciated. Those people, more than others, need to be told that their work is valued.

"Seeking Coaching Is a Sign of Competence"

The more ability one has, the more one can benefit from coaching. Professional tennis players have full-time coaches; weekend amateurs don't. World-champion chess players attend tournaments with an entourage of coaches and assistants. When a game is adjourned overnight the competitor huddles with his advisers, seeking an analysis of his play and suggestions for the morning. The competitor could easily beat these assistants in a game, but that doesn't stop him from listening very closely to their advice. He knows that even though he is a stronger player, they may have noticed something that escaped him, or had a flash of inspiration that eluded him. The same is true in a business context. Far from being a sign of weakness, seeking advice shows a drive to improve and the wisdom to seek new ideas.

"Anyone Can Coach Anyone"

We are wrong to assume that coaching should flow in only one direction: downhill. There are some things that a subordinate knows more about, or is in a better position to observe. And there is always one topic that a colleague knows more about than you do. You have to imagine how you appear to others. They see it. Just as a fan in the stands sees something about a baseball player's swing that the batter himself doesn't notice, your secretary knows more about your tone of voice when you're on the phone with a customer than you do.

Anyone in the hierarchy — superior, equal, or subordinate — may have a valuable tip for you. Someone whom you privately consider less capable may have good advice. Be open to listen to anyone, and evaluate their suggestions on the merits rather than on your opinion of the person who gives it. Since you are the one who will be changing your behavior, it is up to you to decide whether and how you adopt a suggestion. However, the more skilled those offering their observations and suggestions are — no matter whether they are your subordinates, your colleagues, or your boss — the more likely it is that you will make some change.

THEN LEAD: ENCOURAGE OTHERS TO OFFER BETTER FEEDBACK

How do you encourage the establishment of better skills and assumptions about feedback in your organization? Especially if you are not in charge? Luckily, the answer to that question is relatively simple. In the first place, you can offer appreciation to your subordinates, your colleagues, and your superiors. They will likely appreciate it, and the practice is infectious. Volunteering to coach your boss, especially in an organization where that is not routine behavior, is more risky. You will have to be more thoughtful.

Do Something: Request Coaching

The best way to create an atmosphere in which coaching is shared is not to put someone else in the hot seat, but to volunteer to take it yourself. You can encourage others, whether bosses, colleagues, or subordinates, by asking for their observations about your performance. A request for coaching will have the most impact on people at your level or below. If you want your subordinates to ask for feedback from their subordinates, the best thing you can do is show them that you are willing to do so as well.

It will be easier for them to comply if you set a discrete topic for their comments. "How am I doing?" is an awfully hard question to answer. "Do you have any suggestions for me after watching my performance in that client meeting?" or "Do you have any ideas for how I might have handled the pricing issue more effectively?" is much easier to handle.

Don't stop after asking for advice. Listen carefully for what you can learn. And let others know when you've learned something new. The best encouragement you can offer is to follow some of the advice that they give.

Offer Direction: Tell Them What Sort of Feedback Helps You

An easy way to inculcate coaching skills is to tell your colleagues what sort of advice helps you. If you say, "Feedback should always be offered according to the following principles," they might easily hear your comments as an attack on them for having previously done it differently. If you frame your suggestions as the best way to help *you*, then your suggestions reflect only your own foibles. "I have trouble concentrating on improving my work right after I'm told that I'm doing a

good job or a bad job. Could you give me some specific suggestions instead of just giving me a headline judgment?"

Once they begin using the techniques described here, they
will likely find them helpful. The next time they sit down with
a different colleague to offer advice, they will remember the
structure you suggested. If they have no other framework in
mind, your advice may be used by default.

Offer a Diagnosis: People Take Their Cues from Above

If you ask for coaching, your example will have some impact.
Your boss likely casts a longer shadow. Her example will be
more powerful.

Your boss would probably like to have her employees learning more from one another. You can offer her one reason why
they might not be. "People around here look at you to know
how to act. If they never see you ask for advice, they might
think that they should not ask, either." If she agrees with the
diagnosis, then she will have a good reason to ask publicly for
coaching. The advice she hears might help her as well. Giving
her a reason to ask for advice from someone else will probably
be safer than telling her she is doing something wrong.

PART C.
PUTTING IT ALL TOGETHER

8 USE YOUR PERSONAL SKILLS SYSTEMATICALLY

In the preceding five chapters we have offered some basic elements as a way of improving your ability to get things done, alone or with others. We have also suggested a few simple tactics that can be used to stimulate others to use those same skills jointly — namely, asking questions, offering ideas, and doing something that sets an example. These tactics come in handy when you are faced with an unproductive meeting or some other obstacle, and you need to figure out what to say or do. But they do not add up to a strategy. Yet the strategic guidelines that the elements suggest for any task are fully applicable to the task of moving with your colleagues toward better collaboration:

- Formulate your PURPOSE in terms of results to be achieved.
- THINK systematically from data, through diagnosis and direction to what to do next.
- LEARN from your experience by starting early and reviewing often.

- Become fully ENGAGED by taking on a challenging task.
- Offer and ask for FEEDBACK on what works and what to do differently.

We have heretofore avoided mixing "asking, offering, and doing" with "purpose, systematic thinking, learning, and so on" for fear of confusing readers. The same elements can be applied to any task and in many ways once you are familiar with them. While you are still trying to learn them, however, it can be confusing to read about them in different contexts. Perhaps the best way to get others to *adopt* the advice organized around the five elements is to *apply* that advice as you pursue the task of getting them to do so.

This chapter briefly addresses how you, as an individual, can apply the elements of getting things done to the task of getting others to use those some elements.

PURPOSE

Formulate your purpose in terms of results to be achieved by different times. Whatever the size of the organization or group of people with whom you work, you will want to formulate the purpose you will adopt. You will want to set tangible goals for yourself at different points in time, starting with small, easily achieved ones and building to an inspirational vision of a changed organization.

Consider the following example.

In five years the firm will be using the following specific practices:

- Using PREPARE — ACT — REVIEW.
- Having everyone participate in formulating goals.

- Having everyone get regular feedback from coworkers (such as once a week).

In two years those within my department will be doing the same.

In three months my office mate will have adopted those practices and we will be using them together.

You can take the smallest goal and break it down further:

In three months my office mate will be doing a bunch of new things.

In one month we will agree to offer feedback to each other for fifteen minutes at lunch every Friday. In that session we won't worry about each other's egos; we'll just give advice on what works and things to do differently.

Today she will agree to give me some advice on things that she thinks I could do a better job on, and I will react in a way that encourages her to try again.

This example is intended to offer illustrative specificity. Your own set of goals may look very different. They will depend on your personal situation. It should not be too hard to find an inspiring distant goal. Developing an ability to change the way you and others work together is inspiring in itself. And to the extent you succeed you will get the rewards of working in a more stimulating environment.

Try to have your interim goals worthwhile in themselves. (Getting everyone in the office to read this book might be useful but is probably not a good mid-term goal — many people read books without it having any result in terms of their behavior.) Try to focus your goals on results — on actual changes in the way something is done. Finally, try to end up with near-term goals that you can start working on this afternoon, or tomorrow morning, or at the very next meeting you have with others.

THINKING

There is no single tactic that is best for every situation, just as there is no single medicine that is best for every disease. Before you try to lead others toward a better formulation of your joint purpose or toward better joint thinking, you yourself will want to think systematically about the facts, about causes of difficulty, about a general strategy of what you might do to help overcome those difficulties, and what lateral leadership step you might take next.

Think systematically from data, through diagnosis, to direction, and then what to do next. Start down in Quadrant I with the carefully observed facts about how you and your colleagues have been working together. Look at things that are working well, and try to figure out why that is so. Look at problem areas and try to understand what may be causing the difficulties. Figure out what needs doing in broad terms that should overcome those difficulties and move you in the direction of your goals. Then decide what to do next to achieve your most immediate goals.

One of the difficulties you may encounter is that your coworkers may have quite different ideas about what the obstacles are. Some may, in fact, see you as an obstacle. A major part of "thinking" is to develop the habit of stepping back and systematically considering the situation you face instead of reacting to disorganized facts in a disorganized way.

LEARNING

Learn to keep learning from your own experience. As you try to do a little lateral leadership, you are likely to find that it doesn't work as well as you hoped. Before throwing the ideas away as useless, examine other possibilities.

Perhaps these ideas are not as good as we think. Still, it is hard to judge an idea on the basis of one failed attempt to use it without a critical eye on the skill with which it is executed. If the approach we have laid out is quite different from your usual behavior, you will have a hard time making it part of your repertoire. Give it time. Try to improve your skills before deciding that these ideas don't work.

Imagine that you want your boss to adopt different behavior. You try the technique of asking a question to get him to examine his methods: "Do you think we might switch to reviewing the results of sales calls every day rather than pursue the present policy in which we wait several months — by which time we have often forgotten what was said?" Your boss gets red in the face, frowns, and tells you to get back to work.

Before you decide to give up trying lateral leadership, consider some possible explanations for the failure:

- It is foolish to try to get any boss to change.
- There may be ways to get people to change, but not in this book.
- This particular person is not open to learning.

Or, some other possible explanations:

- Asking this question this way was not the best approach in this case.
- My skill at asking questions may need some practice.
- Some other lateral leadership technique might have worked better.

Whenever you try one of these tactics and it doesn't work, look closely at what happened and ask yourself, "Why? What are some possible causes?" Before accepting the easy out that the case is hopeless, we urge you first to look for explanations that you can do something about. Sometimes (after an explanation and permission of the other person) you might be able to tape yourself trying to use a lateral leadership skill. Or you might later write down as much of the conversation as you can recall. Although turning a conversation into a written record is hard, it gets easier with practice. And the rewards can be large. Rather than letting you easily blame others, even a rough text focuses your attention on what you said and what you can do differently. Chess players know that the quickest way to improve is to record the moves of their games and pore over them looking for better moves they could have made. The same technique will help you.

If you practice and regularly review, a year from now your lateral leadership skills will almost certainly be much better. (And by that time you will probably have learned how to do still better by going beyond techniques that we have suggested.)

ENGAGEMENT

Adapt and define your role until it is one in which you become fully engaged. This whole book is about a role we are offering to you. We wanted to sketch a vision of what you can do — of who you can be — in your office or factory or agency. We find the role attractive. Perhaps we are merely projecting what we like to do. Our careers have been devoted to inventing and clarifying ideas for us and others to use, and to teaching others more effective behavior. We've been successful in that task, and we wanted to pass on our thinking so that you could have the same satisfactions and could continue on for us. But maybe this role is not one that you would enjoy playing. That in itself is valuable information for you.

If we are wrong in thinking that you would like this role,

why? What interests do you have that our proposal doesn't meet? Does the role of being a lateral leader strike you as being too lonely? Too much of a solo performer as you try to improve group behavior? If the role we have crafted doesn't appeal to you, you can start thinking how you might adapt it. Perhaps you would become more fully engaged if you found a colleague with whom you could take on the task as a fully committed team activity. Or what else would give you a more exciting challenge every morning?

Figuring out what more you want will also help you offer others more of what they want. If you find something that we've left out of our account of what people want from their job (in terms of the feeling of involvement that it gives them, rather than the financial rewards), then you know something additional to offer others when trying to stimulate them to be better at getting things done together.

FEEDBACK

Routinely express appreciation and ask for and offer coaching advice. Every aspect of trying to influence those with whom you work to be better at working together can be difficult. Even if you do it perfectly it may not succeed. And the odds are that you won't do it perfectly.

Don't merely examine your performance by yourself. On every aspect of your attempts to improve the way a group works together, you have a chance to learn from others. Ask them how they reacted to your attempts to be helpful — from the way you formulated your purpose to the way you offered feedback — and why. Ask them if there was anything in particular you did that turned them off. Asking for feedback is both doing something that can serve as an example for others, and inviting ideas about how you could improve your lateral leadership skills.

9 WHAT IF YOU *ARE* THE BOSS?

This book is focused on the problem of getting things done when you are not in charge. It suggests how those with limited authority can improve the way people work together to accomplish results. But what if you *are* in charge? Has this book any relevance for you?

We, the authors, think so. We hope that executives at any level will find suggestions about individual skills that may help them become personally more effective. We hope that the book may help them envision a future in which members of an organization are better at getting things done together. And we hope that the book will suggest to a leader with authority, methods of leadership that will help move those within an organization toward that better vision.

In brief, having authority does not preclude someone's doing anything suggested in this book. On the contrary, having authority and having status should make it both easier and more effective to implement any of those suggestions.

WHAT'S THE PROBLEM?

No matter how successful a business may be, the problem facing you as an executive is, "Can we do better, and if so, how?" The results produced by your subordinates are not as good as they could be. Part of the problem is that they are not as competent at coordinating themselves as you would like. You have to spend valuable time helping them iron out problems between coworkers. You have to manage them because you can't trust them to manage themselves. There seems to be little you can do about it. You can increase output by investing in better plant and equipment, but it is hard to get your people to be more productive. Perhaps you are not doing as much as you might to improve it. Why?

POSSIBLE DIAGNOSES

There are three possible explanations for why you are not helping improve the collaborative process as much as you might.

- Since your primary goal is to get work done, you focus your attention on *substantive work*.
- Since more than others you have authority to make decisions, you focus your attention on *decisions you have to make*.
- Since more than others you have authority to tell people what to do, *you tell people what to do*.

All three possible causes suggest that you might be wise to focus more attention on the *way* you and others work together, on the *way* you make decisions, and on the *way* you influence people to do things.

SUGGESTED APPROACH: FOCUS INCREASED ATTENTION ON HOW PEOPLE COLLABORATE

To Get Better Results, Pay More Attention to the Way Your Staff Works

Rather than just monitoring the quality and quantity of the work that gets turned out, you may want to spend more time monitoring how everyone is dealing with the elements discussed in Chapters three to seven.

Do people clearly understand the *purpose* of their efforts in terms of results that ought to be achieved by various dates in the future? Have they participated in the formulation of those goals, particularly the immediate goals that they themselves are trying to attain?

Are people *thinking systematically* from facts, to causes of success or difficulty, to strategies for going forward, and finally to the specific actions that they are going to take tomorrow? Are people contributing to that thinking, and sharing it?

Are you and your colleagues *learning from experience* by integrating your planning with your execution? Do you get into action soon enough? Do you pause and review the results of your efforts often enough to learn from them both for their immediate relevance and for the future?

Are your colleagues stimulated and challenged by their work sufficiently to become actively *engaged* in what they are doing? Do they understand that part of their job is to think of ways to improve what you all do and how you all do it?

Do your colleagues generally understand the desirability and satisfaction that comes from supporting one another with *feedback* that includes appreciation, coaching, and advice, up, down, and laterally? Do you have a climate in which such feedback is easily sought and offered?

Such an analysis of the working environment can help people with authority assess a current situation and identify particular areas where attention to process might be most usefully directed.

To Make Better Decisions, Involve Others in the Decision-Making Process

There is no doubt that those with authority also have duties. You have the responsibility to make many decisions regarding the allocation of resources among competing needs and demands. Time and again, the buck stops with you. You can neither delegate a decision down nor kick it up to higher authority, such as a board of directors.

Without delegating or avoiding responsibility, however, you can often improve the quality of a decision and almost always improve its acceptability by involving in the decision-making process those who will be most affected.

Here a simple slogan is: "ACBD — Always Consult Before Deciding." Whether or not the quality of your decision will be changed, a decision will almost always set better and be implemented more readily to the extent that those affected know that their views have been taken into account, directly or indirectly. Of course, not everyone can be consulted on every decision. For many decisions, however, where time and issues of confidentiality permit, questions can be asked widely, well in advance, ideas solicited, and drafts circulated for discussion and comment. A boss can make clear that he or she is not delegating a decision or submitting it to a majority vote but rather seeking input, data, and advice.

To Improve Collaboration, Lead by Asking, Offering, and Doing

Without giving up any of your authority, you can often influence subordinates more effectively by example than by dictate. Model the behavior you would like to see. To be sure, your authority makes a difference. When you *tell* someone what to do, it has far more impact than when an equal does the same thing. Because your status makes telling a more effective strategy for you than it is for others, it is tempting to use this strategy without considering your alternatives. You do it because you can. You can easily miss the fact that your status makes other methods more effective for you as well.

For example, you will also usually have more impact than others when you *ask* a question, *offer* a suggestion or an idea for consideration, or *do* something else that you would like others to do. And often those techniques of lateral leadership will work better for you than issuing orders.

This book contains a great many suggestions of constructive things that a member of a group can do without superior status or authority. On the facing page are two lists. The first offers some of the things that a lateral leader can do without authority. The second list suggests what a CEO with full authority can do. These lists suggest why we, the authors, think this book has relevance for those who are in charge. In fact, it may be more relevant for them than for those who are not.

SOME THINGS YOU MIGHT DO TO IMPROVE THE WAY YOU AND YOUR COLLEAGUES GET THINGS DONE TOGETHER

Without Authority, You Can:

Improve your personal skills at getting things done:

- Formulate your purpose in terms of results.
- Think systematically from problem through diagnosis to strategy and tactics.
- Learn quickly from experience by starting action soon and reviewing often.
- Become fully engaged in a challenging task.
- Help create a climate of mutual support and feedback, up, down, and laterally.

Pursue the organization's goal jointly using those same skills. Work toward that goal by:

- Asking good questions.
- Offering data, ideas, suggestions, and advice.
- Modeling the behavior you would like to see.

Treat those with whom you work as colleagues who may have better data and ideas.
Remain open to different ideas.

With the Authority of a CEO, You Can:

Improve your personal skills at getting things done:

- Formulate your purpose in terms of results.
- Think systematically from problem through diagnosis to strategy and tactics.
- Learn quickly from experience by starting action soon and reviewing often.
- Become fully engaged in a challenging task.
- Help create a climate of mutual support and feedback, up, down, and laterally.

Pursue the organization's goal jointly using those same skills. Work toward that goal by:

- Asking good questions.
- Offering data, ideas, suggestions, and advice.
- Modeling the behavior you would like to see.

Treat those with whom you work as colleagues who may have better data and ideas.
Remain open to different ideas.
AND:
You can make decisions no one else can.
You can order people to do things.

10 CHOOSE TO HELP

There is a story that a skeptic once challenged the famous Rabbi Hillel, "Recite the whole Torah while standing on one leg. If you can do that, I will admit the wisdom of your faith." The rabbi replied, "Do not do anything to anyone that you would not want done to you. That is the Torah. The rest is commentary."

Of course, the wisdom of great sages overshadows prosaic advice about how you can do a better job of getting people to work together. The reason we use the story here is that the skeptic had a pretty good point. He did the rabbi a service by challenging him to boil his teaching down to a single maxim, a maxim that would be:

- Easy to remember.
- A beacon to steer by when interpreting all the other, more complex, ideas.

While our advice in this book is nothing so profound as the rabbi's, we will try to give the reader the gist of it in a brief phrase, "while standing on one leg":

Choose to help.

If you remember none of the detailed advice or careful analysis, you can still remember that message. If you make "Choose to help" your motto, you will never go far wrong.

CHOOSE TO HELP

When others sit by and do nothing as time is wasted or foolish choices go unchallenged, you can be the one who tries to do something. In 1966 a New York apartment building was full of people who were awakened by the screams of a woman being attacked in the courtyard. Dozens of people turned on their lights and looked out the windows to see what was going on. Each of them assumed that someone else would call the police. Nobody did. Her attacker came back later, found her still there, and killed Kitty Genovese.

It is easy, even natural, to behave that way. Although the consequences are rarely so horrible, the same dynamic gets played out in every organization every day. It happens every time we sit through a meeting that is going nowhere. It happens whenever we notice a job that no one is doing, and then avert our eyes, doing only what is assigned us. We hope someone else will do something; they hope we will do it. But nothing happens.

You can choose to get involved. When you see a need you can do something instead of waiting to see if someone else will. You can be the person who tries to do something to save a meeting, to save your division, or to save your company.

CHOOSE TO *HELP*

Wanting to make a difference doesn't mean you have to behave as if you were in charge. Taking over and issuing orders is not the only alternative to doing nothing. Choosing to help means letting others join you in pulling the load. It means not just developing and using your own abilities, but helping them develop and use theirs. Your reflex need not be to take command, but to ask good questions, advance some ideas, or start doing what needs to be done.

WHY SHOULD I?

As a reader, you may notice the hortatory tone of the preceding paragraphs; the authors are discussing what *they* wish you would do. You will be forgiven for asking, "What's in it for me?"

This book asserts that everyone — well, almost everyone — wants to have a job that he or she finds challenging, one that enhances self-respect and encourages the respect of others. The authors believe that taking on the role of improving the way people in an organization collaborate is just such a job.

Bored at work? You will find the task of choosing to help fresh and challenging. If you are now a broker, an engineer, a nurse, an executive, or an assistant, deliberately trying to improve the way people work together is probably quite different from what you do every day. At the same time, you have been a person long enough to have all the expertise about people that you need to start. And there is nothing in your job description that precludes you from doing so.

Are you concerned that what you do does not matter? If you can promote better habits of group interaction you could be the most important person in the enterprise.

And you need not worry. You will never run out of challenging work.

We all operate on the basis of assumptions: assumptions about who we are, what people do, what is appropriate and what is not, what is a good way to spend our lives, and so on. You have to make working assumptions. You cannot choose to have no assumptions. But you can choose what assumptions to make. To stimulate thinking about what assumptions you would like to make, here is a list of two different sets of assumptions.

WE CHOOSE OUR WORKING ASSUMPTIONS
Which Ones Should You Choose?

Some Widely Held Assumptions	Some Different Assumptions You Can Adopt
Problems are someone else's fault.	Perhaps I can make a difference.
There is not much I can do to change the way others behave.	The easiest way to change the behavior of others is to change my own.
Whatever I try probably won't work.	Only by trying will I discover what works.
If it didn't work before, don't try again.	Thoughtful persistence tends to pay off.
Trying to do something I am not good at may be embarrassing.	Everybody learns new skills by trying things they are not good at.
Some of these ideas are useless.	I can adapt some of these ideas and find them useful.
Some things have never looked worse.	There has rarely been more room for improvement.
The world is basically a terrible place; in the end we are all dead.	It's more fun being an optimist.
I don't have to get involved.	The more involved I become, the fuller a life I lead.
I can get away with looking the other way.	I can choose to help.

Our final point is this. Look at these two rows of assumptions. Which set looks more fun? Which would more likely lead to an interesting, satisfying life? Which assumptions make you feel better when you read them? The authors' advice is to pick that list and mark it up a bit until it becomes a set of working assumptions that you are prepared to adopt.

Then adopt them — at least for the time being, until you find better ones to choose.

Appendix

Preparing to Lead Laterally

Perhaps you can see sense in applying the approach described in this book but are concerned that you will not be able to do so well enough. It seems risky, especially until you have used it sufficiently to be skilled in its use. You can't carry the book around with you and keep referring to it. Nor is it possible to keep all the details in mind all the time. So what can you do to try out the approach without too great a risk?

You can see any change from a habitual way of doing things as risky. The question is how best to limit that perceived risk. One way is to feel that you are well prepared. If you feel that you have prepared well to do something, you are more likely to do it. And there is no risk in preparing. It just takes time — time that can prove well spent. Yet we have all taken considerable time in preparing for a meeting but felt unprepared once it starts. So what is being well prepared? What is "good" preparation? The purpose of this appendix is to help you carry out the type of preparation that will assist you to get things done together with others. It will help you prepare well to use the ideas in this book to lead laterally.

No author can know the precise details of a particular job or situation that any reader needs to tackle. What is clear is that if you work in any organization, large or small, private, public, or voluntary, you will spend much of your time in a variety of different groups. In some, you may meet with just one colleague, a subordinate or your boss to tackle a particular difficulty that has arisen. In others, you may be a member of a project group or working party. In others, it may be a departmental or management group meeting. All these groups come together to get something done. They need to do so as effectively as possible, and then break up so their members can go off to other situations. In those, the subject matter will be different, but the need to collaborate well will be the same. The advice that follows can be adapted to help you prepare for any situation where you come together with one or more people and want to get something done as effectively as possible.

Whenever there is a need to get something done, one or more people are likely to identify that need. They may then do some work on it before inviting others to join with them to carry it further. Some of the preparation that you can do will depend on whether in a particular instance you are an "initiator" or a "joiner." Some will be the same in either case.

Preparing to Lead Laterally As a "Joiner" If You Have Little Time

Before going to any meeting where you will be collaborating with one or more people, how can you best prepare? Even if you have the time — and you probably will not — it will only be confusing to re-read the whole book. So what are the key ideas it will be helpful to have clearly in mind before you get to the meeting?

Whatever your role or position, whatever the situation in which you want the collaboration to get something done to be effective, there are three questions to ask yourself.

What will indicate that collaboration is effective? If a number of people are collaborating effectively there will be many indications. It would be very difficult to try to keep in mind and watch for all of them. What you can do is look for how the five basic elements of getting things done are being handled:

- PURPOSE — Whatever the situation being tackled, those involved, including you, will only be able to perform effectively if there is a common understanding of the purposes being pursued.
- THINKING — No group will be working effectively unless all members are "thinking in sync," systematically.
- LEARNING — If the group is effective, it will move forward through "cycles" of Prepare — Act — Review, with all helping to integrate thinking and doing.
- ENGAGEMENT — If collaboration is good, all will be fully engaged in contributing both to the job in hand and to improving the way people are working together.
- FEEDBACK — There will be an atmosphere of mutual support and coaching. People will build on rather than dismiss each other's efforts.

How do you work out what has to be done, what "nudge" is needed, if the vision of good collaboration in any of these elements is not being achieved? Having this vision in mind will help you to observe more systematically. Of itself, it will not tell you what has to be done to influence and improve the situation if your observation indicates that the vision is not being met. Alan remembers meeting someone who had attended one of his training courses some weeks earlier. Since the latter had seemed to derive considerable benefit from his experience on the course, Alan was surprised to be greeted with "That course was a disaster!" The reply to "What on earth makes you say that?" was "The trouble is that now I can see all the things that are going wrong with every meeting I attend!" Systematic observation alone is not enough. It is also necessary to think systematically about what is observed (DATA) through underlying cause of the difficulty (DIAGNOSIS) to what has to be done in general to overcome it (DIRECTION) to specific actions to do so (DO NEXT).

How can you give that "nudge"? Once you have observed that collaboration is less effective than it could be in relation to one of the elements, how can you contribute to bringing about improvement? In the body of the text, we suggest that three basic techniques are:

- To ASK a question.
- To OFFER your own thoughts and invite others to build on them.
- To DO something that will serve as a model.

You need to use these basic techniques to reach the point where some specific action is taken to overcome the cause of the observed difficulty. Their value is that even if you cannot get beyond the observation of a difficulty (like the course participant above), you can still do something to help. You can offer your observation and ask others to build on it by suggesting possible causes of the difficulty, then proposals as to what should be done, and finally specific action to do it. Thus, you can guide a joint effort to work through the stages of the Circle Chart on page 79 to tackle the difficulty. Alternatively, you may judge that it would be more helpful, if you can do so, to work through the Circle Chart on your own before offering a detailed proposal, or even taking action yourself to deal with the difficulty. The following page shows five examples, one in each element, of an observation of a difficulty being progressed through the four quadrants of the Circle Chart to develop a specific action to tackle the likely

	QUADRANT I OBSERVATION (DATA)	QUADRANT II POSSIBLE CAUSE (DIAGNOSIS)	QUADRANT III WHAT HAS TO BE DONE (DIRECTION)	QUADRANT IV PLAN (DO NEXT)
PURPOSE	People seem to be talking about different topics	They have different purposes in mind	Clarify and agree the purposes to be pursued	List different suggested purposes. Build into an agreed statement over three points in time
THINKING	Some people are putting forward plans while others are still trying to establish facts	They are at different stages in the thinking process	Get everyone thinking in step	Ensure everyone stays in step by making clear at all times at which stage we are in the thinking process
LEARNING	Every time we get close to doing something, someone brings up an alternative possibility	There is a reluctance to take the risk of trying something in case it does not work	Weigh the risk of continuing to delay with that of testing the suggestion	Whenever anyone puts forward a suggestion of what to do, ask: "What's the risk of trying it?"
ENGAGEMENT	Several people seem to have switched off	They were unable to get into the discussion because others were doing all the talking	Ensure everyone has a chance to contribute anything of relevance they have to say	Give everyone a chance to gather their thoughts in silence. Then go round table to hear all contributions
FEEDBACK	People's suggestions are being ignored or "shot down" as unworkable	The relevance of suggestions and possible ways of developing them are not being considered	Check for meaning and relevance of every contribution	If the relevance of an idea is not apparent, ask for an explanation rather than allow it to be ignored

underlying cause of the particular difficulty. For ease of presentation, they are shown in columns rather than in four quadrants of a circle.

No matter how short a time you have to prepare, it helps to remind yourself of:

- The five basic elements, as an aid to what to look for.
- The Circle Chart, as a method of organising thinking to come up with ways of overcoming any obstacles to collaboration.
- The basic techniques of ASK, OFFER, DO, as ways of providing a "nudge".

Taken together these form a complete system for applying lateral leadership, and the more you become familiar with them and their use the easier you will find it to do so. No system can be a substitute for judgement, but the more you apply it the better the judgements on applying lateral leadership you will make.

Preparing To Lead Laterally As a "Joiner" If You Have More Time

Your boss or a colleague has asked you to see her to help tackle some specific job or situation. She has no time to give you any information about it in advance. Your first impression may be that you can do nothing before you see her. That is largely true as far as the content of the job is concerned. Obviously, the general preparation as suggested above, to help make collaboration effective, will be useful, whatever the job may turn out to be. If you have the time, is there more you can usefully do?

Presumably you will want to contribute any relevant facts or ideas you have for getting the specific job done. You cannot do so unless you have a clear understanding of what the job or situation is, what needs to be achieved in tackling it, and the PURPOSES for which it needs to be tackled. Therefore, you will need to ensure that you have a common understanding of these with the boss or colleague who has asked you to help and any others who you may find are involved. For example, if you have some idea, however vague, of what the job or situation is, you can consider what the purposes are likely to be. You will then be able to OFFER your thoughts and check with the initiator that these are in line with hers. If you have no idea at all of what the job is and cannot come up with any answers, you will need to consider how best to ASK a question to ascertain what the initiator may have in mind. The point is that if you and any others involved are to collaborate effectively, you know that a set of results to achieve together needs to be formulated. You will want to help bring this about. It will assist you to do so if you have thought about it in advance — even if it is only as you are on your way to the meeting.

Second, you know that if there are a number of people involved their thinking will not automatically be "in sync." There will be a need for some methods or procedures to help keep everyone in step. These will help to ensure that the VISION for the THINKING element — all those involved "thinking 'in sync,' systematically" — is achieved. It is possible that the initiator will have some proposals for methods or procedures aimed at this. If not, how will you give a lead? This may depend on what people consider normal ways of working in your organization. For example, if it is common to use a flip chart or whiteboard, you might OFFER a proposal of using it to gather ideas and thoughts in an organized way through the stages of the Circle Chart. You might even decide to DO something to illustrate its use. You are more likely to do so if you have thought about it in advance. If such practices are not common in your organization, you will need to think about other methods. Perhaps you can try to keep everyone thinking "in sync" by ASKING the relevant questions at each stage and making it clear when a move is appropriate from one stage to another. Again, you are more likely to do so if in preparation you have thought clearly about the vision you wish to bring about and how you might do so.

Third, getting things done involves doing as well as thinking. Moreover, it involves integrating thinking and doing so that you move forward, trying things out as fast as the risks allow, and LEARNING from the experience. The VISION you need to have in mind is of everyone helping to integrate thinking and doing. To bring this about, you and those with whom you are working need to follow cycles of Prepare — Act — Review both in the way you are tackling the particular task and in the way you are collaborating. How can you bring this about? For example, you might look for ideas or suggestions put forward by others that seem to be getting lost and ASK what the risk would be of trying them out to see how they work. You might OFFER the proposal of a short break to review and suggest improvements to how you are collaborating. Again, if you have thought of possible ways beforehand you are more likely to do something.

Fourth, you know that if a number of people are working well together then the level of ENGAGEMENT is high both in the job itself and in trying to improve the way they are collaborating. The VISION you want in your mind as you prepare for the meeting is one of all those present being fully engaged. That means they will be contributing facts, ideas, and suggestions and offering to do things on the job in hand *and* suggesting ways of improving collaboration. In your preparation, consider how you might encourage this. One thing that helps to generate enthusiasm is being enthusiastic yourself. So think of things you might DO, whether on the task in hand or on improving collaboration, where you can set an example. Another thing that encourages engagement is to take up ideas and develop them. Resolve to listen for what is potentially useful in anyone's suggestions and attempt to build on it. If you do, you will almost certainly find the opportunity!

Fifth, if your collaboration goes well there will be something noticeable about the content of the FEEDBACK that people give and the way they give it. The VISION you want to create is of an atmosphere of mutual support and coaching. How can you encourage this? You can resolve to draw attention to at least some of the helpful contributions of others as they happen. You can also make a point of looking for and making a note of examples of when the meeting made good progress (for feeding back in any review or to an individual after the meeting) and who did what to bring this about. Again, if you have thought about this in preparing for your meeting, whatever the topic, you are much more likely to do it.

Preparing To Lead Laterally As an "Initiator"

If you are determined to lead laterally, there is much useful preparation you can do before any meeting, even when you have not initiated it. But what if you are the initiator? Obviously, you need to consider what you will do to manage the same elements. It will be helpful to remind yourself of the possible ways of doing so suggested above for "joiners." It will also help to remember that your preparation needs to take account *both* of the content of the particular job you need to tackle *and* of how to make good use of the abilities of those joining. As the "initiator," you will have more knowledge of the content of the job because you are raising the need to tackle it. That means you are able to do more work and thinking on it. However, that very ability raises important considerations. Your preparation should involve judging at what point in your own thinking you would prefer to start to communicate with those who will be joining you. The further you go, the less opportunity there may be for those joining to provide the relevant facts, experience, and ideas they have in determining what has to be done and how to do it. If you have already worked out what is to be

done and how to do it *before* communicating with those joining, they may well feel that they are just required to carry out
instructions; that their own ideas (which might have influenced
what was to be done and how to do it) are not required or welcome. Consider the difference if you begin to communicate at a
point where you are clear on just the broad purpose to be pursued and perhaps what has to be achieved in very general terms.
Then those joining will be able to contribute toward defining
what has to be achieved more precisely, establishing what has to
be done and planning how to do it.

So what should you take into account in making this judgement? Some factors are:

- The time available before you have an opportunity to
  communicate compared with that available for completing
  the job after that point. If the latter is short, you may feel
  the need to go further to ensure the job gets done, and
  those joining will be more likely to understand this.
- What you know of the skills, experience, knowledge, out-
  look, and interests of those joining, and their likely willingness to help and level of commitment to the purposes
  being pursued.
- The balance between ensuring as good an outcome as possible on the particular job and encouraging contribution
  from those joining on that and future jobs. If this is a situation where you have a continuing relationship with those
  joining, for example if you are a manager and these are
  your subordinates, you may be concerned to guide or steer
  the meeting in such a way as to encourage and coach them
  to develop their willingness and ability to contribute more
  fully in the future.

Having done whatever thinking you judge appropriate on the
content of the job, turn your attention to how to make good use

of the abilities of those joining you. You have reminded yourself of ways of managing the five key elements suggested above for "joiners." Is there any further detailed preparation you can do? Those joining may well expect you, as the initiator, to put forward some ideas for managing the meeting. Most meetings have some sort of agenda to keep everyone focused on the same subject matter at the same time. A meeting concerned with getting something done may have only one topic, but it is clear that there will be several stages in tackling it. It helps to be clear in your preparation what those stages are and how each will be handled so that everyone is going in the same direction and stays in step.

You know that whatever the situation is there will be a stage early in the meeting when you will wish to ensure that those joining have the same understanding as you and as each other of:

- The situation to be tackled.
- The purposes to be pursued.
- The sort of outcome and quality required.
- Any other relevant thinking or work you have already done.

This stage will be followed by one where relevant information — including facts, experience, and ideas — is gathered.

There will then be a stage of considering that information, including diagnosing the underlying causes of any difficulties or obstacles.

Further stages will follow to establish and ensure common understanding of:

- What has to be done and the priorities.
- Plans for *who* is to do *what* by *when*, even though the detailed methods may be left to the individuals concerned.

These stages can provide a useful rough agenda or structure for the meeting. Experience shows that for the proceedings of any meeting to go smoothly, it helps also to follow some understood procedures or methods at each stage. These should ensure that everyone has the opportunity to contribute and stays in step in their thinking. As the initiator, you should think about what procedures you might propose. Alternatively, you might consider whether you will invite those joining to suggest procedures to follow. You should also consider how to manage the available time effectively, including establishing and keeping to a rough timetable.

To sum up, leading laterally effectively as an "initiator" is a matter of balancing the need to get things done with getting the best out of each individual and with the encouragement of cooperation and teamwork where several are involved. It requires observation of the whole "wood," how people are thinking and feeling, how they are interacting, without losing sight of the "trees," the job itself. The simple checklist on page 84 should help.

Finally, if you are in a position of greater authority than those joining, remember that the more *you* choose to apply the method and principles of lateral leadership, the more likely *they* are to choose to help and apply them.

Analytic Table of Contents

Roger Fisher, director of the Harvard Negotiation Project and Williston Professor of Law, Emeritus, at Harvard Law School, is one of the world's leading authorities on negotiation. He has advised negotiators and helped broker peace agreements in business and international politics from South Africa to El Salvador. He lives in Cambridge, Massachusetts, USA.

Alan Sharp has been a senior manager in the electronics industry and an executive director of the Coverdale Organisation, an international training and consultancy firm. He has worked as an independent consultant in the UK, USA, and Scandinavia, and has trained senior executives in business, government, and international agencies in building effective teams. He lives in Essex, UK.

'Roger Fisher's previous co-authored book, *Getting to YES*, of which I bought dozens of copies, was one of the most useful published during my lifetime and sold over three million copies. With its larger ambition, this book may do even better. It is must reading for those seeking to maximize their contribution to the constructive work of the world ...'
Charles T. Munger, Vice Chairman of Berkshire Hathaway Inc.

A highly useful, clear, no-nonsense guide to successful persuasion and influence. It should become the best friend to managers, professionals, and ambitious working people everywhere.'
Rosabeth Moss Kanter, Author of *World Class* and *Rosabeth Moss Kanter on the Frontiers of Management*

'To get the work done today, you must be able to collaborate. Roger Fisher and Alan Sharp have provided the best road map I have seen for collaborating, navigating, and leading your way through ambiguity and unclear lines of authority.'
Philip J. Harkins, President and CEO, Linkage Incorporated

'Fisher's done it again! He and Alan Sharp have produced a terrific guidebook, chock full of practical wisdom for those who must lead in today's world, from any position, with and without authority, through collaboration. Profound lessons made simple by one of the world's great teachers.'
Ronald A. Heifetz, Author of *Leadership Without Easy Answers*

'This timely, practical, skill-based book beautifully answers the typical seminar complaint "This is good, but the person who really needs it is not here". It'll inspire you with the power of example, clear thinking, and the tools to pull off successful, sustainable collaboration with or without formal authority.'
Dr. Stephen R. Covey, Author of *The 7 Habits of Highly Effective People*